Buddhist Guide to Manifest Parallel Realities

Using the Four Noble Truths and Eightfold Path in the Age of Consciousness

Von D. Galt

Copyright © 2016 Von D. Galt

All rights reserved. This book, or ebook, or parts thereof may not be reproduced in any form, stored in a retrieval system, or transmitted in any form by any means – electronic, mechanical, photocopy, recording, or otherwise – without prior written consent and permission of the author except in the case of brief quotations in articles and reviews as provided by the United States of America copyright law.

While the author has made every effort to provide accurate information at the time of publication, neither the publisher nor the author assumes responsibilities for errors or for changes that occur after publication.

Please, consider requesting that your local library branch purchase a copy of this book.

ISBN-13: 978-1530171354

www.VonGalt.com

Cover designed by Von D. Galt

Dedicated to my little brother,

Medta Douangphrachanh

whose incarnation as a handicapped boy has taught his family more about themselves than they could've learned without him in our lives.

CONTENTS

Introduction 1
Chapter 1 Noble Truth #1 Life is Suffering 14
    Suffering is Physical Pain 15
    Suffering is Emotional Pain 17
Chapter 2 Noble Truth #2 Attachment Causes Suffering .. 22
    Attachments are Addictions 25
    Attachment to Expectations 28
    Attachment to Forms 31
    Attachment to Things 36
Chapter 3 Noble Truth #3 Insights Remove Suffering 38
Chapter 4 Noble Truth #4 Living the Eightfold Path Ends Suffering 44
Chapter 5 Eightfold Path 50
    Correct Thought 51
    Correct Speech 53
    Correct Action 56
    Correct Livelihood 56
    Correct Understanding 59
    Correct Effort 63
    Correct Concentration 64
    Correct Mindfulness 67
Chapter 6 Applying the Principles 73
    Matrix of Delusion Worksheet 82
    Examples 85
Conclusion 190
About the Author 213
Index 214
Bibliography 215

Introduction

"You yourself as much as anybody in the entire universe deserve your love and affection."
—Siddhartha Gautama

Reality is a mirror to re-teach you love.

Lesson reminders are everywhere. If you have become "conscious", then you have become self-aware of your reality. By doing so, you may have experienced first-hand that some things and people in your everyday reality have changed that you can no longer pretend didn't happen or gloss over it as you've done time and time again. For instance, some people who are conscious have noticed people, especially celebrities that they vividly remember have passed away and all the sudden they are still alive.

Maybe you even noticed a brand-new large building in a lot that you regularly walked by and it was not developed before and know that this new building couldn't have been there yesterday. Some of you may even notice that your associates have more or less children than you previously remembered them having. Some current events and possibly some natural disasters you remember occurred in one manner have also changed in different ways. The houses and cars of people you remembered having may have even changed as well.

So, what the heck is going on? Am I going crazy? No, you are not. Your conscious has teleported to a parallel reality that matches your new energy frequency based on a decision you made that changed your perspective on a life lesson you just learned from. Your reality and all the people and circumstances you experience now are real. I recommend taking them seriously so you can continue to manifest better and better experiences for yourself to engage with.

Quantum physicists are exploring evidence of parallel realities as more and more people become conscious to explain this phenomenon happening worldwide to many people. Until full evidence is realized, then what do you do with this newfound conscious way of life? You my friend have become conscious and become a self-aware, enlightened human being. Once you walk through that door, you cannot go back to being asleep.

Now, you can start to really play with the matrix. You can now begin to understand what all the enlightened teachers of the past and present have been talking about in texts now and through the ages regarding how your decisions and wisdom you earned changed your reality. Pay attention and you'll have a more enjoyable ride. There is nothing, but love.

All creations of fear and negativity are roadblocks to remind you that they are illusions covering up the energy of love. Polarity is just an instrument in this reality used to reflect love back to itself. Hide and seek, there you are. If you get anything out of this book, it is this. You are not just loved, but you are love. As love, you are the cause and everything outside of you is the effect. Suffering is optional.

Everything and everyone is made of atoms that vibrate at different frequencies. Those different frequencies make up all the form you experience in your reality. When you change your own frequency by radiating at different levels of consciousness, you become the spinning marble that attracts everything else around you to change in the blink of an eye. You did not change anything, but yourself. And as a changed particle, your consciousness, which is the soul living within your body is teleported into another version of you in another reality that already pre-existed at that level of vibration and you just moved and integrated your other consciousness in this new reality.

Like all the sudden, you had an epiphany over something you have been musing about for a long time and became even more self-aware. Consciousness integration is a continual process. The whole point of continuing to integrate your consciousness is to learn and grow from your experiences in the matrix and evolve spiritually so you can qualify for new higher levels of consciousness by meeting the pre-requisites.

Your soul yearns to grow and expand and life is the instrument in which it can do so. Your soul does not stop once it finishes a life journey. It may rest in the spirit world, but eventually, it wants to get back on the cycle of life and rebirth to continue its journey to grow and expand. Your soul planned its next incarnation and set of lessons in the spirit world. Upon birth, your conscious forgot the plan and the answers to your lessons.

Conscious amnesia allows you to test yourself to see if you truly learned the intended lessons without the answers given to you. The universe is an ever growing expansive library of archive lives of people, animals, planets, and cultures with a plethora of new experiences to learn from.

Enlightenment is just being self-aware of the matrix you exist in and becoming a more conscious co-creator of your reality. There is no end game to creation and you were not just created energy to be here to accept creation and call it quits when life is over. Energy is eternal. There is no beginning and no end. Just changes in form. Noticing slight differences are the challenge you have to become more self-aware of the changing external environment and integrate your consciousness into the existing version you are in now to become more of yourself. Assessing what perception about yourself and what recent incident sprung the new perception that saw the same situation differently is what changed your frequency.

My definition of spirituality is not how often you attend church, say and do any rituals, and so forth. That's just religion. Personal growth and wisdom through interacting with the universe is what spirituality is. Spirituality is a personal journey to grow and learn from your experiences and use that knowledge to create more satisfactory experiences for yourself and God to enjoy through you.

Mystics are people who are aware of these universal principles in the universe and know enough to engage with it more consciously in their creation of their universe they experience. Mystics come from all traditions, religions, and walks of life. There is more than one way to become enlightened. That is why there is no point to argue with other paths and convert anyone. Those actions are just making a circle for yourself. When you are ready to jump off the circle to be a more self-aware manifester in your spiritual journey, then the wonders of the universe and the playbook is at your fingertips.

Your unlimited and ever-reaching journey to co-create with the God has begun. The universe is your playground. God is the creator of you and given you the ability to create whatever experiences you want so God can experience itself through directly experiencing your personal growth. Metaphysics are the teachings taught by many master teachers throughout time about the nature of our existence and reality.

This book is the teachings of one such teacher, Siddhartha Gautama whose teachings I have been raised to with. Not every Buddhist will have the same understanding of the Four Noble Truths and Eightfold Path as I do. It does not matter the different perspectives of others. What matters are my perception and the journey I create for myself. What will matter to you is your perceptions and how that designed your journey. I am the cause of my reality I affect as you are yours. Siddhartha Gautama was the 1st Buddha that documented the foundational teachings that make up Buddhism.

A Buddha is just an enlightened person and Siddhartha was not the 1st and not the last. Buddha's are anyone that range from men, women, children, and any sentient being who is self-aware of their creations in this planet and even in many other universes. So-called "aliens" are just sentient beings who have come long before the inception of man. Human will evolve to be the aliens of other evolving civilizations. It's all just different forms of God's creations playing different forms to experience itself. The myth that Buddha's are limited to only men is a cultural belief that has been adapted into some people's adaptation of Buddhism, which is incorrect.

Regardless of the person's gender, ethnicity, age, and even species, what your human aura radiates at tells the maturity of the consciousness embodied in that person's body. So, there is no point arguing with people who have separatist and limited beliefs. We are all on our own journeys and to each their own. If the reality they exist in works for them, then love them enough to let them experience their own creation.

This is my interpretation of the basic Buddhist principles taught to me and used to manifest parallel realities from the frequency I radiate. I have tested it out and continue to test is out. I know many Buddhist and people of other faiths who spend most of their lives trying to find enlightenment and an end to the cycle of reincarnation. Only to be surprised when they come back to experience another life when they undergo hypnotherapy to uncover the source of their chosen incarnations and profound life choices. Life is not the enemy. Life is an opportunity to make your life into an enjoyable experience. Being in the image of the universe, God, or whatever you want to call creation is to recognize that you are the spark of the divine and the divine essence lives and experiences itself through you. You, my friend, are God.

Once your consciousness goes back into the spirit world, you get integrated into the whole and bring your experiences and wisdom back so the universe can experience more of itself and appreciate its own creations through you. Think of consciousness as energy. Energy exists and does not die. It can be divided, combined, and made new.

As a divine being made in the image of creation, you are a co-creator of worlds and with your consciousness, you make your world around you. The challenge in this reality experience is to learn from your mistakes and successes and continue to create more experiences for you to appreciate all the different forms that love embodies. You have existed before this form and will continue to exist after this form in many dimensions in time and space and outwards for eternity in this reality, multiverses, in physical universes, and spirit dimensions. The universe played out in your experiences is nothing but children ever amusing itself with the various creations it can imagine to learn, grow, and re-appreciate its creation.

The greatest creators are the ones who can take a bad hand and turn it into a jackpot. Life is nothing but a hologram and you are the game changer. This book is nothing but a guide to help steer clear and defuse any roadblocks you created so you can move to creating better experiences for yourself other than spending your life creating new levels of suffering and re-learning the same old lessons for much longer than needed.

Keep the words in this introduction with you as you read through this book. The introduction is the intersection in the middle of an infinite eight pattern you will journey while going through this book. As you use these teachings to analyze your experiences that cause you suffering, you will see more and more that you are loved and you are love itself. Again, you are the cause and everything else is the effect. Welcome to the ride your soul intended you to go on. May your ride be wicked!

Chapter 1

Noble Truth #1: Life is Suffering

"The mind is everything. What you think you become."

                             –Siddhartha Gautama

     In Buddhist concepts of suffering, it is the measurement of pain. Suffering can be understood as a variety of things we measure, but in all, it is relevant to the slow aging process of practically everything in this reality and the emotion associated with experience. Life is not without suffering, but we can choose to live with less pain in this journey. Plain and simple, suffering is pain.

Suffering is Physical Pain

The act of living is a slow aging process that over time the slow aging process of years of usage and degeneration of the body brings on growing pains. These pains such as aching backs, tired knees, failed organs, and many other forms of slow degeneration of the body are tell-tale signs of suffering that the body is communicating to the host soul as pain. The pains felt are the way many people use to measure how their body is aging as compared to before they started to feel such growing pains. A great example of a physical pain all of us feels is stress.

When someone is highly stressed out from taking on more than their body can handle, then their body starts to show the pains of induced stress. From my observation, stress can induce illness such as weakening people's immune system and making them more susceptible to catching colds and flus more easily and it can prolong the recovery time. Stress can show in cosmetic ways by bringing on hair loss, acne, and turn your hair gray. It even can bring on migraines, neck pain, and a variety of other physical ailments. Stress even brings on mood swings and short temperaments that charge emotions.

Charging these emotions with toxicity brings on a response by the universe of more of the same. I've observed people age physically at much accelerated rates on people who live very stressful lifestyles. Some at 40 years old can look 15 years or older than they should be. At the same time, someone who is the same age that lives with less stress and also manages their stress better have aged much slower and look much younger than their age states on their driver's license. Every moment is filled with choices. These choices can be of ease and synchronicity or filled with hardships and stress. There is a give and take in all our choices and the cause and effect from such decisions produce the pain seen and felt physically.

Suffering is Emotional Pain

Pain is also felt on an emotional level. Throughout our lifetime or as many Buddhist believe in reincarnation, many lifetimes. Once we are born into this chosen life, we begin our lessons towards hopefully, spiritual evolution by participating in a series of experiences that bring emotional dramas. The emotion felt in all experiences by people are the way the universe measures growth. Emotion is the energy that the universe measures. People radiate an aura that records their spiritual level of consciousness. When someone experiences something starting off from their infant life experiences, it produces an emotion.

For many infants, hugging and embrace from their parents evoke an emotion of safety and love. As a result, infants who feel these emotions flourish at a faster rate than infants that do not get much affection. On the flipside, many people also start feeling the 1st taste of negative emotion that they have to process when they are rejected, hungry, or a series of other experiences that do not produce that loving feeling that infants recognize. These are the beginning experiences that induce a set of emotions that babies begin to grow from.

As we mature over our lifetimes, these loving and non-loving emotions become more sophisticated and complicated as the person experienced more depth in their interactions with other people and the physical environment, they live in. To understand this, "emotion" is best recognized as the movement of energy. Remember, emotion is the only measurement that the universe can measure in someone and their progress to learn from the experience is the building block of the next set of experiences that person is manifesting. People can not escape negative emotions. The human experience is one of polarity.

In order to learn the positive lesson, the person must have experience in what the negative outcomes could be. For some, other people's negative experience is enough to learn from. For many others, they must have first-hand pain associated with the experience to truly have the muscle memory of the effects of the negative memory burnt into their psychology. How someone deals with those negative emotions and resolves issues become the foundation of the negative experience that shows if the person has learned what they need to.

It may also limit the amount of negative experiences they project for themselves or show that they need more of the same types of experiences or even worst experiences to learn from. The universe is always gaging how much of the lesson does this person need and can handle in order to learn the lesson. The universe is unbiased to positive and negative emotions. It just responds to what you send out and gives you more of it.

Understanding the basics of suffering will greatly help you in understanding how you as a co-creator with the universe manifest your experiences to learn from. Remember, every experience has emotion. The positive emotions do not age you as much physically and do not get weighed by time. Time flies much faster when you are happy and having fun as compared to unhappy and not having fun. The negative emotions are the toxic energy you send out to the universe that ages you physically and slows time.

You cannot escape suffering as life itself has its own set of experiences that have some pain involved with it. It is designed that way to help you see your choices and make better choices so you can reduce the amount of suffered pain you feel and live more in joy. I will expand on the techniques to address your suffering later in the book. For now, just know that life is suffering and suffering is physical and emotional pain.

Chapter 2

Noble Truth #2: Attachment is the Cause of Suffering

"We are what we think. All that we are arises with our thoughts. With our thoughts, we make the world."

−Siddhartha Gautama

Now that you understand the basics of suffering, you are ready to move the next thing related to suffering. All suffering is caused by some attachment to what is not working for you in your lived experience. All attachments are forms. Forms come in many different shapes. It can be in the physical form of things, in the form of a pattern, in the form of expectations, or in the form of an addiction to emotions, and many others we create. I will explore these common types of forms.

This attachment to trying in so many different ways to make something work for you and the result not getting it what you expect is causing your suffered pain. Addressing the source of the believed outcome you have that you are attached to will shorten the pain you suffer from continuing to live with this grieved attachment and get you on your way to manifesting in a more smooth process through synchronicity than forced actions you can conceive of. I understand that there are experiences in life that are out of our control. This is a matter of your beliefs in reincarnation or not.

In Buddhism, the philosophy believes in reincarnation as a soul's chosen pathway to try different lifetimes and situations that test its ability to learn and grow from those experiences. Some experiences are very troublesome and many question why a soul would choose such a perceived horrible experience. This again is up to the soul to resolve and I would recommend seeking past life, life-between-life, and future life hypnotherapy to understand why a soul would choose such difficult experiences to learn from. For the purpose of this book, I can offer the abbreviated reference on how to manifest using these techniques.

Deeper answers to philosophical questions about your chosen incarnation and experiences are part of the life journey and I would refer that those answers could be found in hypnotherapy. The source of the attachment and the resolution to address it will be explored in the Eightfold Path section of this book. For now, we will understand what attachments are and get a strong grasp of it.

Now, let's explore all the different attachments that I have observed. I'm sure once you get started in familiarizing yourself with this process you can start uncovering all the different attachments people come up with to cause self-induced suffering within their control.

Attachments are Addictions

Attachments itself is a form of addiction. Understanding the source of why people are addicted to something is the beginning to living and projecting experiences correctly.

Unfortunately, many people create experiences from unconscious addictions to an attached belief they have in themselves and what outcomes should be like. This attached addiction continues the cycle and is believed in Buddhism to repeat in karma lifetime after lifetime until the soul finally learns from the source of what is causing the attachment and begins to create properly. By doing this, they balance out their karma. In short, karma is a tool to reset unbalanced energy within the person.

Exploring the source of the attachment, resolving it and moving forward to manifest correctly will balance the energy of the person and manifesting out of bad habits can be stopped. Once you understand attachments are addictions, and then you can begin to see how people are addicted to drama. Some people live in and thrive in drama. If their lives are not filled with drama, then they will create it for themselves. The outcomes of dramatic melancholy are attention and support from intended parties, punishment and ridicule, feelings of self-worth, and a variety of other emotions the person feels from this experience.

When someone is addicted, they are addicted to the emotion they feel in that high that the addiction brought them. For example, drug addiction is an attachment to the temporary high the user experience which evokes an illusion of love and positive vibes, while damaging the person's body and livelihood in the meantime. The source of substance addiction is an attachment to the positive emotions the user feels when they are under the influence that they seem to think only exists under the drug use and not found in life. It's an escape mechanism to addressing the source of their personal pain either physically or emotionally. The struggle for recovered addicts is to continue to self-diagnose their life choices that make them susceptible to substance abused and make better choices for themselves living a lifestyle which is free of the elements that reinforce substance abuse and surrounding themselves with a supportive environment living in the same clean manner.

    Anyone who has ever gone through a 12-Step program for addiction of any kind knows it is not easy to live with a sponsor and keep yourself clear from your own inclination to use again. If all of us had a coach to check us when we steer down the abusive path of attached addiction in life, many of us would not enjoy that level of self-reflection every day. Maybe this is why life coaches are growing as a profession. In short, drama queens suffer from self-created illusions of depravation when they set-up experiences that create tension in their lives. They are addicted to drama.

Attachment to Expectations

Another common attachment is an addiction to pre-conceived expectations. Many people have an image of how things are supposed to end up or what needs to happen in order to get what they wanted out of the experience. Often, these expectations are from comparing the results of what others have gotten from similar experiences. If they pursued a relationship, a career, a friendship, a regiment, and so many other things people pursue and it does not turn out as they expected, then they get upset.

It's not the experience that they are upset with, but the failed expectations they had held at the beginning of the decision to enter into that situation that they had that did not fulfill what they thought was going happen. So, many people try many different avenues in the same experience to try to get a new outcome with the hopes that a new outcome will happen. If it doesn't result in what they wanted originally, then they are disappointed and they create the emotional energy of lack, dismay, anger, and many other negative emotions they feel about the failed outcome. What the person has failed to understand is that you must make the decision and make the needed actions towards the desired experience and then let go of your attachments to how the outcome should be like.

This removed any negative energy you create in the form of emotions that send out hesitation, pause, waiting, longing, and any other emotions relating to holding a thought for an expected outcome. This is the energy the person sends out and no wonder they get more stop signs and pauses on their experience aside from a quick manifestation. When you let go of the attached outcome you expect and let the universe set things up for you, it will send the quickest set of events that fall right into the path you needed to take to get to the outcome for the original decision you choose. You will be surprised that the outcome the universe delivers is often much more desirable and easier than you could ever come up with on your own.

There could be a reason why you didn't get that opportunity because a better opportunity was in line for you. The closed door could also have prevented you from a bad experience. If you are co-creating with the universe, then the universe will put things in place that is of ease for you to do at the right time and place. You just have to be in the place of mind to be open to seeing it when it happens and take action on it. If you hold onto an expectation, then you are closing off on the many ways and shorter ways you can get to the desired experience.

Attachment to Form

Attachments to forms are a very common one. If you look at your life and the lives of many people, you will see we all have a routine in everything we do. We have grown accustomed to that pattern and it becomes a habitual behavior after we repeat it long enough. When these patterns are disturbed and changes, many of us will deal with it differently. The thing is we need to accept that change is the only thing that is constant.

In Buddhism, one of the basic exercises they do is to draw very elaborate, beautiful mandalas with sand that takes a long time to achieve and then destroy it to show you are attached to the form that resulted from the work. People get disappointed and sad when they destroy it, but it is a very effective exercise to show how easily we are attached to form. On a deeper level, form can only exist when time is measured. In Buddhism, we call this plank time. It is where every second of a person moving is like a slide show that documents a series of movements. You take one slice of the moment and you have the form of the person in a position. You put the series of movements together and you have the action of walking.

The gathering of form in action is time and that's how we measure the progress we make in order to see ourselves making the decisions we made for personal growth. In essence, time is a self-created concept for measurement in this dimension. When you understand the attachment to form, then you begin to realize that time does not exist and all things exist at the same moment. When you review a decision in your life in relation to time, then you can feel the emotions of appreciation, resentment, despair, growth, and many other emotions that help your soul learn.

Here's the kicker, the soul is energy and energy does not cease to exist. It will just change form. Your soul is energy that has consciousness. Energy is equal to consciousness. So, you can't feed the soul a cheeseburger and it will be happy forever. What feeds eternal energy are growth, joy, satisfaction, and all the various ways we can label the emotion of love. Your soul wants to realize and feel more of itself. Your soul wants to exist in the energy of love. The energy of love permeates in the spirit world and existing in the physical world, it wants to feel that energy as well through your personal, spiritual growth that these life lessons offer.

All negative emotions are just a tool to help you understand your lack of love and push you to address the core issues of attachment causing your suffer pain so you can return to a state of living in love. The only emotion that is real is love. In Buddhism, the universe or as many religions call God is love. Everything is love and there is nothing, but love. All souls are a split of the divine consciousness. When you understand that energy can be isolated in small amounts and can be combined, then you can see that each soul is a divine speck of the larger consciousness of the universe. This is what Buddhist call spiritual emptiness. The zero point is where we all come out of and where we all return. Every journey out of emptiness and returning back into emptiness brings new insights for the whole. This is the meaning of oneness in terms of energy and the cosmos.

The individual experience is for spiritual growth and that spiritual growth is reviewed by the soul when integrated back into nirvana where the one consciousness resides. As made in the image of one consciousness, you can create any way you want. This is all an exercise to rediscover love, which is the only energy that exists. In Buddhism, there is a mythological belief in some cultures in Lombardo, which is a form of so-call hell, but when the user understand the attachments to form that bring them to create such as illusion, then the illusion disappears and there is nothing but consciousness or God however you want to understand it. There is nothing, but love. Other common patterns that people are attached to are a pattern for a relationship. They have enjoyed a friendship, romantic relationship, familial relationship, or a career pattern for a certain way for a long time.

    Suddenly it seems that the relationship has changed and that pattern no longer exists. Change has happened and many people deal with change differently. They try to push for the old pattern to return or adapt to it or move on from it. The thing with change is that it is best to enjoy every moment of a pattern you like and be grateful for it. When changes happen, access the attachment that is causing your suffering and begin to create new experiences. Accepting what is and letting go of what hasn't worked is adaptation. These techniques of acceptance and letting go will be explored further in the application section of the book.

Attachment to Things

Attachments to things are one of the forms that many people can understand easily. Things are already a physical form. People get attached to such things as cars, houses, their body image, their hair, and so many other physical forms. These forms are energy put together to create a shape that functions for an intended purpose. For instance, a car is for transportation as is using your body to walk. When a car is no longer needed, the physical parts can be melted down into the bare minerals and reshaped into other things.

On a granular level, those minerals are all open spaces in the molecules and the only thing existing is the energy holding those elements together to maintain that molecule. The same concept goes to all physical forms. More luxurious cars and houses, for example, are products of more elaborate forms that people place a perceived value on.

Chapter 3

Noble Truth #3: Insight Removes the Cause of Suffering

"Peace comes from within. Do not seek it without."
—Siddhartha Gautama

The issues that continue to surface in our everyday lives are the effect of what we are projecting out of ourselves. In Buddhism, the foundations for reality as a mirror of our projections are based on the concept of cause and effect. Simply, you, the co-creator of your reality are the cause. Everything and everyone else mirroring back your projections are sheer manifestations of your beliefs you have about yourself and about life. In essence, the reality you interact with is the effect you, yourself caused. You are the cause and everything outside of you is the effect.

What prevents people from fully understanding how and what steps they choose that got them into the dilemmas they suffer from arises from a lack of subconscious, limited, or refusal to gain insight into the causes of their suffering. When you break down the matrix of your illusions to get an honest assessment of how things transpired, then you see where and why you choose to make the decisions you did that lead up to the situations you suffer from currently. Insight, my friend, is not always kind to your ego. Your ego will push away the cruel and honest truth, make up lies, and prevent only a limited portrayal of the elements that make up your conundrum. When you check your ego and assess the situation from all points, then the only thing that remains are the basic elements of the hard truth of your reality you created for yourself from yourself.

Until full insight into the nature of your view of yourself and your ability to use the projections in your life experiences as living mirrors of your belief about yourself and about what lessons you need to learn from such experience are fully taught, then you will continue to manifest much of the same hardships and struggles. You can read all the books you want, chant all the hymns and mantras you see, align yourself with all the spiritual rhetoric and religious dogma you seek, but until you actually live and learn to manifest correctly from within, then your exterior reality will only return more of what you send out over and over again. One karmic lesson to another to another. Lifetime after lifetime. Until you stop the endless cycle of manifesting more pain and suffering for you to finally learn from.

Once you learn to create properly, then you can limit the pain you suffer and shorten the learning curb by manifesting smoother and more quickly. The extra steps are just teaching tools you needed to learn in order to get to the final phase of that desired experience. Some people do not need extra steps to get to the same outcome because they already learned what they needed earlier. There is no end to your journey as when you complete one journey, and then you begin another journey at a different level.

Insight into the nature of your own reality is what your soul desires you to know so you can halt the repeatable suffering. As I said before, you are the cause and everything else outside of you is the effect. Since insight removes the cause of the suffering, then insight to see that you are the one standing in your own progress by manifesting your subconscious beliefs you hold about yourself and the world you experience. You manifest the world you experience on a daily and localize level, but as your consciousness is also part of a collective consciousness in this shared world reality, then you are a piece of the collective whole projecting out your combined view of reality.

As you begin to understand how you create your own holographic reality from within your consciousness, you will begin to become more aware of your surroundings and the subtle changes that occur in the same people and environment you interact with. I'm not a scientist, but I have learned from my understanding of using Buddhist principles to manifest with. When you change your view of a specific situation by accessing it and gaining insight about it, then you change your energy.

Since the universe can only communicate in terms of energy and vibration, by you gaining insight into your manifestation, you change your energy frequency from lower, slower vibrations of confusion, frustration, and sadness to higher and faster vibrations of joy and love for life. According to the concepts, the change in energy from your human aura does change the reality that is mirroring your beliefs you're projecting out.

It is moving your self-aware consciousness from your body in this reality into another body you have in another existing parallel reality that is already vibrating at that higher frequency. This is what Buddha meant when he explains how reality is a mirror of your thoughts. All people you interact with and all environments have parallel versions in all realities. With that, there is no need to save anyone other than you from yourself. Once you jump from one reality to another and begin to notice slight differences in people and the environment, then it is your challenge to adapt and continue to co-create with the universe a more enriching experience you desire to live through in this lifetime. So, insight really does remove your self-created suffering.

Chapter 4

Noble Truth #4: Living the Eightfold Path Ends Suffering

"He who walks in the eightfold noble path with unswerving determination is sure to reach Nirvana."
　　　　　　　　　　　　　–Siddhartha Gautama

Life is for the living of it. To exist and not live to your fullest potential by creating the best life you get to experience is just passing time.

People can feel much burden by all the baggage they have accumulated over their life and many lifetimes from excessive garbage they self-created and live with as manifestations of their projections from within appear and often reappear. No wonder many people get so tired of living and just want to check out. The option of suicide just puts you back on the wheel of karma to balance out your old, acquired lessons not learned.

In essence, you are trying to balance out old, blocked energy that you have not accepted and let go of the attachments you have held previously. The Eightfold Path is a set of principles that can help you gain insight into how and the instructional purpose behind why you created the manifested reality you experience. Once learned, it is also a set of principles in which you can use to manifest more enriching experiences you prefer to interact in. From my understanding and practice of living with these principles is that it reinforces the notion of cause and effect. Most of the delusions we experience and the pain associated with it is due to people trying to change the effect and not themselves who are the cause of their external environment.

    Now, we get back to the concept of reincarnation a little bit here. The Eightfold Path cannot eliminate set life experiences your soul had originally designed for you to experience as part of the life experiences for you to learn from when it was organized by you in the spirit world prior to incarnation. The parents you choose, the race you choose, the culture you choose, the status you choose, the appearance and health you choose, and so many other elements you choose to have in order to have the form you needed to be equipped for playing out the role and roles you intended to participate in for your over-all soul's growth and evolution.

    Think of it like this. If you want to learn what it's like to scuba dive, then you need to have the right equipment and be in the right location to do the dive lesson. Life is just like that.

I continue to recommend past life, life-between-life, and future life hypnotherapy if you need more in-depth analysis to why you choose the life you experience. The Eightfold Path is just a set of principles for helping manifest in everyday activities for those unfixed elements of your life that are flexible.

As I've mentioned in Noble Truth #1, which is that life is suffering and expand further to explain that suffering is pain felt either physically or emotionally, the Eightfold Path lived can reduce how much suffering you endure. Unfortunately, you can't completely eliminate suffering because life itself is not without suffering. There will be pain associate with aging. It is part of the human experience. In some situations, you can end the suffering by learning the lesson. The pain felt in different aspects of life are reminders that you have tension that has accumulated by not having insight into the reasons why you created the pain that you feel today.

Most lessons are learned through pain. The toughest lessons are the most painful and that pain is burned into our muscle memory and psychology. As creatures of habit and pattern, many people forget the painful lesson and when things get good again go back to starting a new way to repeat the same old lesson to relearn again. Life is a mirror. If you see something that reminds you of a lesson you supposedly learned, then take it as a reminder. Seeing signs like a stop sign is a reminder to look before proceeding in order to avoid any potential accidents. Learn the lesson and try not to repeat it. Once you address the lack of insight that reduces the suffering you feel, then by moving forward in living the Eightfold Path, you will start manifesting more consciously.

As a conscious and more self-aware co-creator of your reality, you will live in more harmony and peace with the flow of life and suffer much less than how you used to manifest experiences from. The effects that you cause will surprise and delight you in how much easier it is to notice opportunities that relate to what you like to act on. Acting on such opportunities will be effortless and enjoyable. That joy will make time fly by and age you much less, because you are having a great time manifesting consciously. If a roadblock occurs, then you know how to access it using the Eightfold Path.

Chapter 5

Eightfold Path

"No one saves us but ourselves. No one can and no one may. We ourselves must walk the path."
—Siddhartha Gautama

The Eightfold Path is quite simple to grasp.

When you understand them, you will wonder,

"Duh! I already know this." So the real question is why aren't you using it every day? The application of the Eightfold Path will be examined later, but for now, let's go over the basics of what I understand the principles to be. Everyone will have a slightly different interpretation and that's just a matter of syntax. These are my simplified understanding of it and it has worked for me in manifesting the reality that matches the frequency I project from within myself.

Correct Thought

      Correct thought is to be self-aware of the thought you are thinking about. When you notice a thought that does not resonate with how you truly feel about something or someone, and then correct it. Uncorrected thoughts fester and build into larger uncorrected thoughts and then when those thoughts produce a situation in your outer experience that are a reflection of your thoughts you have held for a while, then you are seeing that to which you have thought. Many people go about their having many thoughts and many of them are random such as what is on my to do list, what will I eat, etc. Our minds are clogged with random thoughts and we are stressing out our minds with all the jargon we put in it.

Write out your to-do list or your thoughts and get it out of your head so your mind is free of clutter. When a random thought comes up inspired by your experience, an advertisement you saw or a conversation you had and it does not resonate with you, and then reject the thought as not a belief you want to hold onto. For example, if you see an advertisement that suggests a prejudice and you are offended, then don't just let that thought sit in your head to become a belief you hold. If you agree with it and it is something you are fine with, then keep it in your head.

If it is a thought that makes you uncomfortable, then reject it as an incorrect thought and acknowledge it is not something you agree with and believe in. By accessing it at its source, it will not sprout into an underlying incorrect thought capable of mounting into a serial manifestation. If you want to go further, then speak your opinion about that subject to the correct originator of the advertisement. Over time, you won't need to do a lot of accessing and policing your thoughts, because you will have developed a habitual way of noticing thoughts you don't like and rejecting them as not yours to have. The good news is that many people have positive and happy thoughts all day long. So you shouldn't have to reject incorrect thoughts very often.

Correct Speech

Correct speech is talking with the right words that match your actions. Many people can become frustrated with the reality they are experiencing, because they say that they are saying the right mantras and speaking the right things. Yet, the reality is not matching what they say. The thing is, your speech and the words you choose to speak out loud must match the actions and emotions you emanate. If you say you love someone and at the same time, you do something that is hurtful to that person and feel anger towards them if they do not so as you please, then you are not using the correct speech that matches what actions and emotions you are sending out. The correct speech would be to say you do not want to have any connection with that person.

That would match the emotion of anger and the hurt you are doing to them, which would cause a disconnect to occur. If you truly want to have a loving relationship with that person, then you would say you love them and a matching action would be to love them enough to accept them as they are and not shelter them from their own harm that they created for themselves to learn from. You would send well wishes and let them know that you will be happy to help them if they meet you halfway and help themselves, but if not, then you can only offer them good sentiments and well wishes.

Correct speech is not just saying and acting in sync. It is also providing a disclaimer to your actions so people understand the reasoning behind it. Love is not always about rescuing and helping people out. It is allowing people to fail if they continue to seek a harder path to enlightenment and being there to help pick them up when they are willing to start to help themselves and meet you half way. In order to have reality be in matching frequency to the version of you that's projected, you must send out clear instructions.

If you are saying one thing and doing another, then you are sending out mixed messages and will get a little-confused result back. I like to give the analogy that if you say you want chocolate ice cream and stand in the vanilla ice cream line, then don't be surprised if the cashier serves you a chocolate-vanilla swirl ice cream to try to appease your confusing instructions. That's how the universe works.

Correct Actions

The common saying I have heard is that actions are louder than words. That is true. You can say all the best prayers, sing all the hymns and praises, and repeat all the good mantras you want, but if you don't back it up with the same action, then the words are cheap. For instance, if you say you want to lose weight, but do not regularly exercise and live an active lifestyle, then you will not become healthy. Again, if you say you want a happy marriage, but complain and argue often, then you are acting against the words you choose to speak. It's as simple as that. Act in accordance with what you say you want. Act clearly.

Correct Livelihood

Correct livelihood is the act of living in accordance with the reality you want to be part of.

You can only really control yourself and no one else. If you want to live a healthy lifestyle where you are fitter and suffer less weight related illness, then you need to change your belief system that enables you to live a lifestyle that puts out an unhealthy environment. For instance, if you want to be healthy, then the lifestyle you must live is one where you are actively walking, playing sports, eating smaller portions, and eating less fattening foods. These lifestyle choices are a match to a healthier version of you.

You can't say you are a healthy person if you continue to eat fattening foods often, do not do much physical activity, and continue to live out the bad habits you have about yourself that fuel the binge eating. Once you complete the matrix of illusion to uncover the source of the stress in your life that causes the binge eating and why you feel that lack of self-worth, then you can begin to change your core beliefs about yourself and begin to change the lifestyle choices that causes your issues you are experiencing in your environment. For example, Alcoholics Anonymous participants who go through their kitchen cabinets and throw away all their alcohol when they want to clean up have realized that the core issues to their alcohol abuse is escapism from dealing with the stress of life and the feelings of inadequacies. For a binge and stress eater, they will empty their pantry of junk foods when they are ready to eat healthier.

What they are doing is resetting their lifestyle. By changing the different aspects of the lifestyle you exist in, you are changing every little action that make up a lifestyle. If you want to break it up into mini correct actions, then it would be preparing your meals in advance so you have healthy options, brief walks throughout the day, accepting invitations to work-out or doing physical activities after work, choosing to eat smaller meals, etc. As you can see, all these small action steps become a lifestyle change. That is correct livelihood in a nutshell.

Correct Understanding

Correct understanding is simply seeing all aspects of the picture to get a comprehensive idea of why the situation is in the state it is in. I often find that many people who are confused and frustrated by why their reality is in the shambles they are in is due to a lack of perception. They either choose to see what they want to or avoid seeing the issue from other perspectives in order to justify their positioning or they are quick to come to a conclusion without the proper research. This lack of information and insight is the cause of much miscommunication.

For instance, say you are a parent of a disobedient child and do not understand why your child is acting like a spoiled child. As a parent, you begin to punish your child for an outburst and move on, but then the same issue occurs later on. You punish the child again. What the parent does not realize is that they are only putting a Band-Aid on the child by punishing them and the next time, the punishment has to be stronger and stronger because the child has become immune to the last form of rectification. If you take the time to understand how this attitude came about, discuss it with the child and look at yourself as the cause, then you will see that your child is the effect to you as the cause.

You may have had a poor upbringing and decided to spoil your children with all the things and opportunities you did not have. By doing so, you sheltered your child from mistakes that they can learn from, the opportunity to work for what they enjoy and feel gratitude for building good work ethics and understand the value of what they earn as a result of what they put in, and the ability to build good character that other people outside of their family can appreciate.

When you begin to access yourself and how you had a hand in growing the spoiled "monster" you deal with now in this reality, then you can begin to address your issues with deprivation and self-worth and start to have that honest conversation with your child that you will not shelter them from their mistakes, but will do your best to provide them some wisdom and guidance. If they should fall, then hopefully, it won't be as bad and you will be there to support them if they pitch in and do their part. If you have that kind of conversation, then you won't feel angry at your child for being the person you have raised them to be and start correcting your actions from then on.

So, by stopping the gravy train, you do yourself a favor and your child a favor so they can grow to be self-sufficient, successful people full of integrity and character that you want to hang out with when they're adults. Another version of this limited insight in incorrect understanding is to short sight yourself by not seeing fully your part in the picture. Let's say you child is the grown up person who has done a lot to try to have a relationship with you, but eventually they gave up or the relationship became strained. As a result, you blame them for not trying to have a relationship with you in your senior years.

    I find that when the camera is turned on the person to see where they have failed, I see a person who was not always there for their child growing up. This is someone who failed to provide support, affection, and also manipulated their child for their own gain. It was just a matter of time when that child grew up and moved on to focus their attention on their own life they created for themselves. I will get more into these types of examples in the Matrix of Delusion exercise.

    The thing about parent and child relationships is that it's not the responsibility of the adult child to be a companion to their lonely parent. Just as it wasn't their grandparent's responsibility to be that for their parent. Inclusion into the child's adult life is a privilege, but not a requirement. If you love your child, then you will let them grow and watch them grow successfully. Smothering them and keeping them always in your grasp is sheltering them from living their life and is a selfish way of parenting. If that is your choice, then do not be angry at them for not having a fully enriching life of their own separate from you. Your child is a reflection of your inner feelings about yourself. Again, you are the cause and your child is the effect. Your child is the reflection in the pond that ripples when you look in it. If you want the picture of you to change when you look at the pond, then you must change you...not the pond. The pond will never change for you because reality is only a reflection of your perception.

Correct Effort

    Correct effort is the motivation to move towards that which you say you want. You can say the right words towards the experience you want and do the action steps towards it, but before doing any action, you must make the effort when the opportunities that lead to the next steps towards manifesting that reality happens. For example, say you want to make more money to pay your bills.

You say to others what you want to do, but unless you begin to apply for jobs you qualify for and take opportunities to apply for mentorship and possibly apply for additional job training through schooling, then you are not doing your part to put out the effort to take advantage of sending out to the universe the message that you will work for opportunities to manifest this said outcome you desire. Some opportunities to take action may not even come unless you apply yourself. Correct effort is applying yourself and sending out the feelers and messages to the universe that you are committed to finding an opportunity to take action on.

Correct Concentration

Correct concentration is the ability to focus on the prize. Many people will want to experience many things and as they make the journey to set in motion the things that are needed to complete the final end result of a series of action steps they took, they get distracted. It is our easy ability to get distracted from our intended purpose that halts our progress. You must focus on what you want and stay focused on it. Any distractions that you participate in are just reminders that you may not really want what you say you want.

    For instance, a lot of people want to go to school to get the skills and education they need to qualify for a better paying job, but they are easily derailed from staying committed to their regimented studying schedule to instead focus their energy on getting caught up with opportunities to go have fun or get caught up in the dramas of life. Life happens and unfortunate things occur, but sometimes, it is best to compartmentalize your emotions and situation for a time and a place so you can stay focused on your studies.

    When the school exercise is over, then they return to the drama affecting their life. This is an example that no matter what it is we want to experience in life, there will be many distractions. There are only 24 hours in a day and anytime you refocus your attention on other things and other people's dramas, you are stopping the living of your life and part-taking in the living of their life. You have to remember that if you are not living your life and consume by other people's dramas, then how much of your life are you living?

There are drama queens who like to suck other people's time and energy to amplify their own misery instead of fixing it. If the drama does not involve you, then wish them the best with it and let them go to fix it themselves. Otherwise, you may be enabling them by trying to build them up as compared to letting them build themselves up. The later choice is often the one where the lesson is learned that benefits both people. Focus is the continued energy you put into staying on the path you choose so you can manifest your intended outcome.

Correct Mindfulness

Correct mindfulness is just being more aware of something and using that emotional intelligence in how you create your reality. For instance, if you noticed that your neighbor has a regular routine every time they mow their lawn, then you have paid attention to that particular pattern. If you wanted to develop a neighborly friendship with your neighbor so that we can watch over each other's homes, then you would be intelligent to know this pattern that your neighbor exhibits and take an opportunity to water your plants at the same time so you can acknowledge your neighbor by waving at him or her when they look up at you.

Building this routine over time builds a silent and comforting routine of hospitality, which builds a bond of careful attention over each other's homes. Instead of moving on with life in such a fast pace manner, consider slowing down some time to observe the patterns surrounding you. Stop and smell the flowers that bloom. Wave and smile at people when they pass you. Take in all the subtle ways the universe is vibrating different wavelengths. Being mindful is being more conscious of those subtle patterns that make up life and noticing when subtle changes occur. When you notice changes that are different from what you remember they once were due to being more observant of reality, then you become a more conscious and self-aware person.

    The ability to be mindful is your ability to recognize changes in your environment and realize you have quantum jumped into a new parallel reality. If you want to know what you did different to move your consciousness into this version of you, then analyze what you recently did or interpreted a situation you were dealing with differently. That change in perception is what changed the frequency your aura was vibrating at. Your aura is just your chakras and changing the frequency is done by changing your consciousness about any particular thing you were working with. That's how energy is changed.

Here is an analogy to grasps how human energy changes frequency and this changes their parallel reality to one that is already pre-existing in their new frequency. We all know the emotion of anger. When we are angry, we feel enormous pressure to release it either physically or emotionally. If we try to make things happen while angry, things do not always work out for us, because anger is a negative emotion.

All negative emotions have a separating quality and functions independent. That's why people don't want to join up with an angry and negative person. In contrast, if you feel the emotion of acceptance, then nothing can really upset you as you accept it is what it is. You don't try to control it and make it something it is not. You work with what you got and make the best of it. When others come across you and like what you are doing, then they may want to join you in your quest and the energy of unity fuels more of itself. You can always add, but continued subtraction leads to zero.

The reason why is because positive emotions are the energy that combines and unifies. Positive emotions are in essence one emotion of love. All negative emotions are just reminders that you are off balance. In order to defuse the underlying source of that suffering to balance out your energy again, you must access the source of your caused emotional quagmire. This act always returns you to the love energy that creates. In short, love energy creates, hate energy destroys. Negative energy exists as polarity in our reality to help us create by seeing the two sides of our choices and deciding which path we want to create from.

In Buddhism, there is no right or wrong, just different choices that relate to cause and effect. Now when you change your emotions, which is energy in motion. Hence e...motion. You change the vibration level of your energy signature you send in motion. That's how people radiate at different wavelengths. The more conscious and self-aware they are, the more complex and higher vibrating their energy signature that will bring them to greater and greater creations of reality that have more possibilities to create with. People who vibrate higher will raise other people's energy out of default. Like a fast spinning marble that bumps into other sitting marbles and gets them to move faster in the box. If the people do not want to be present with the higher vibrating person, then they will not be present, leave or not communicate any longer.

Frequency is the nature of reality. If you vibrate higher, then you jump yourself into a higher dimension where more people of similar vibration will be. It's simple metaphysics. My interpretation of the word "meta" is that it is a short term for "self" or a "reflection of self". My interpretation of "physics" is the study of how things work. So, the study of "metaphysics" is the study of how you work and create. Here we are again, you are the cause and everything else is the effect. You are the person who created the ripples in the pond that you look at. If you want to change the pond, then you must change the person looking into the pond. A mystic is someone who is mindful of the nature of reality and creates consciously from observing the patterns in their reality. Correct mindfulness is the act of being conscious of your surroundings so you can use it to create with.

Chapter 6

Applying the Principles

"However many holy words you read, however many you speak, what good will they do you if you do not act on upon them?"
                         -Siddhartha Gautama

I spent much of my young life watching my

parents and their friends at Buddhist temples

praying for the answers to their problems and

listening to the teachings of the Buddha. Over and over they sit and listen, but go home and repeat the same painful lessons. Many of the problems are self-created and I believe it is a lack of knowing how to apply the principles of the Fours Noble Truths and Eightfold Path that many are seeking.

Once the path is understood and applied, I still see many people re-create the same lessons with new painful situations over and over again. I think it is that the ego of the person is stronger than the conscious soul sitting in humor watching the ego's creations spiral out of control. For us to have an individual experience and grow wiser from our painful experiences, we are all given an ego that has an identity. We all know better and know what we should do, but we do not listen to our consciousness tell us what we should be doing. Instead, we listen to the grumblings of our ego.

To humble yourself is to allow your ego to exist and co-create with your higher-self. Your higher-self is your conscious soul who sees the fastest and most amusing way to create your next experience from. You cannot get rid of ego. To do so would be to get rid of the individual experience we choose by incarnating here. Life is like a labyrinth and the ego allows us to not see the answers to our own chosen paths. There would be no growth if we knew the answers. It is the journey to seeking and finding the answers to our problems we create that provides the food our soul's desire.

Again, we can't feed the soul a cheeseburger or a veggie burger. It thrives on finding love. It likes hide and seek. Creating experiences to undercover the love under that gunk you create provides your soul the joy it seeks. You'll understand what I mean by this when we do the Matrix of Delusion exercise. As creator of habit, I think many people resort to their old patterns, because they do not know how else to live differently. They do not know how to create a new life for themselves. When someone uncovers the source of their suffering, then they must decide if they want to continue to live as they have in that manner or learn a new way to create the reality they live in. Pain is the best way for many of us to learn our lessons. Pain is attached to learning.

We can read something and learn from it, but many people will remember the lesson if it has a hard, painful memory attached to it. So, pain is a reminder for many of us to steer away from the bad habits we have done that created our suffering. Many people will say that they want the suffering to stop in their lives, but run away from seeking the answers that are the root cause of their creations. To be brave enough to see the source of your suffering and create from the Eightfold Path is a journey full of excitement and joy.

There will still be suffering as life is not without suffering as lessons are attached to pain, but you can limit the pain you suffer by learning to be a quick learner. In these exercises below, you will see the Four Noble Truths and Eightfold Path play out over and over again. The exercise will continue to peel away the layers until you get to the bottom of the issues and see the belief system you have that has brought you away from the only truth in the universe. The universal truth is you are loved and you are love itself. You are love playing peek-a-boo with itself.

The Matrix of Delusion worksheet is a simple breakdown of the Four Noble Truths put into a four-part formula. I use the word "delusion", because when someone completes the worksheet, then they can see where and how they have been holding onto a limiting and often one-sided perspective about the issue that is contradictory to what the logical perspective is. Hence, the person has been delusional about the situation and by refusing to analyze all angles to see how the suffering was created, take responsibility for their part in creating it, seek resolutions, and act on those solutions, and then they have let the issue fester into more and more suffering.

Often, there can be layers of issues that have mounted up before the person finally has suffered enough pain to start chipping away at the problem. What the Matrix of Delusion does it help to take an objective approach to an issue that someone is trying to understand and break down the components in a logical manner. It requires full honesty in answering the questions. What you may find interesting is to allow others to fill out a worksheet regarding the same issue to see the full aspects of how the issue was created by the person. The solution is application of the applicable aspects of the Eightfold Path to prevent the recurring lesson from unfolding again and again in so many varying ways.

By completing the worksheet and getting clarity, you then change your perspective on the same issue you have been trying to work with using the same level of consciousness. Your energy changes when you change your perspective. Your human energy pattern of frequency changes when you energy changes. According to the metaphysics (studying how self-works) in Buddhism, it explains that once you change your perception, then reality changes to match your frequency. You did not change reality. Your consciousness just moves into another living version of you in the already existing parallel reality that radiates at the new frequency.

You just integrate your consciousness to the one you just became aware of by noticing slight changes in your reality. This act is what consciousness is and what the whole idea of enlightenment, awakening, Christ consciousness, and whatever terms we want to use to explain the ability to be aware of our reality and be more in control of how we manifest experiences. That is why in Buddhism, there is no need to have missionaries and try to convert people. We know that everyone is having the experiences they have chosen at a conscious level or a higher level for their soul's advancement.

Experiences that are more deep in nature such as someone's born handicaps, parents they chose, nationality, family members, and other more serious experiences outside of one that people self-create in their daily lives to suffer from are a higher level manifestation that Buddhists believe have a soul purpose that may be related to karma to balance out lessons not learned in previous lives or a difficulty that is pre-designed by the person's soul that is a lesson that will help advance the person and those around them spiritually. I advise the person seek a quality hypnotherapist to regress them into the past life, life-between-life, and future life hypnotherapy to ask those questions to their consciousness while in Delta brain waves.

    Your consciousness is your unconscious while you are awake. This is when you can lie to yourself, but you cannot lie to yourself when you are asleep. That is because your soul or higher self is the consciousness that is present in your dreaming state and it does not tell lies to you. If you are able to be hypnotized, then you are a patient that can have your hypnotherapist ask questions to your consciousness regarding these deeper questions about your incarnation. Your consciousness will show you why you have this incarnation and what the intention that these lessons were supposed to achieve.

Now for the everyday suffering that people self-create that can be a small issue or overtime mount up to a very large issue, the Matrix of Delusion worksheet can help remove the blocks that people have put up to help remove the self-inflicted dramas they are dealing with that can be removed. The real key to using the worksheet and applying the Eightfold Path is to not re-create more drama for yourself when life starts to settle into a peaceful balance. This is where "living" the Eightfold Path can be hard for some people who actually thrive in suffering.

As I have stated earlier, suffering itself can be an addiction. The worksheet can address that too. I've found that drama queens addicted to creating suffering enjoy the attention and healing they get from it. It is also boredom in not wanting to find new interests that lead to going back to old patterns of manifesting drama. Now, let's get started.

Matrix of Delusion Worksheet

The formula is broken into these four aspects.

Suffering | Attachment (s) | Cause(s) | Lack of

1. Life is <u>suffering</u>.
2. <u>Attachment</u> is the cause of suffering.
3. Insight removes the <u>cause(s)</u> of suffering.
4. Living the <u>Eight</u>fold Path ends suffering.

<u>Suffering</u>: List the things that make you suffer or in other words that you are unhappy with?

Attachment (s): List the "perspective" or "expectation" you have with what is that doesn't work for you? Be honest or your just wasting your time.

Cause (s): There are reasons (causes) behind what is. Understanding the causes brings insight and clarity to how it was conceived.

Eightfold Path: They are correct thought, correct speech, correct actions, correct livelihood, correct understanding, correct effort, correct concentration, and correct mindfulness. People experiencing the same reoccurring issues lack living some aspect of the Eightfold Path. Over time, applying it regularly will become an automatic habit and way of being.

    Completing the exercises for each issue you are looking at will bring insight. Insight removes your suffering. By living the Eightfold Path, you end your suffering or at the very least, reduce the amount you suffer. That's the formula for the Matrix of Delusion. Now we will apply it in many examples I have come across that I think are very common in many people's lives. These are some suggested examples and concepts I've come across, but you could find more for the specific situation you are trying to analyze. The point of the exercise is to get you familiar with how to complete the worksheet and apply the clarity you get into your lives.

      These are the basics to understanding how to use the Four Noble Truths and Eightfold Path in everyday life situations you are trying to find clarity on so you can resolve them and move forward without such drama holding you back. These interpretations are my understanding and how I have come to understand the situations I have come across in my life from direct experience and from those I love.

      Applying this exercise will help you change your frequency by getting insight into the causes of your suffering and by seeing the same thing differently you move your consciousness into the matching frequencial reality where the new circumstances resonate at that new vibration. Enjoy your ride and go along with it. There is a reason why you are experiencing the reality you're in. Remember, you are the cause and everything else is the effect.

<u>Examples</u>

Suffering #1:

My spouse doesn't spend time with the kids and me anymore. He's or she is not able to fulfill social commitments. I need a break from the constant household duties when he/she gets home. My spouse nags me when I get home from work to complete the long list of chores.

Attachment (s):
- I'm attached to the perspective that he/she should validate me 24/7 because my worth is through someone else.
- I'm attached to the belief that the man needs to provide for the family and be the model of a perfect husband and father according to the nuclear family structure I was raised in. He needs to be able to balance his commitments to spending time with us, perform church activities, and the other commitments he has. My job in this modern era is to be the dutiful wife and home-maker no matter if the kids are in school most of the day and we're living on a limited budget.
- I'm attached to the expectation that my spouse needs to spend free with me and the kids so we can have a relationship regardless of the excessive hours my spouse works to support us.

- I'm attached to the expectation that I must be the vision of a perfect housewife and keep everything looking spotless even though I can't keep up with my extensive to-do list.
- I'm attached to the image of being a perfectionist and doing everything thoroughly even though it takes more time than I have to complete each task from scratch.

Cause (s):
- He/she works extra hours and sometimes a couple jobs to make enough money so we can afford our lifestyle.
- You have unrealistic expectations about how detailed things need to be in order to meet up with your perfectionist standards. Regardless, if it exhausts yourself, your spouse, and the kids, your perfectionist

beliefs stem from a need to be accepted and accomplished.
- You spend more than your spouse makes. Living beyond your means is making him/her work more, which doesn't provide time to fulfill commitments.
- He or she is overscheduled trying to make you and everyone happy. He or she rarely gets enough sleep and has no personal time. These unrealistic expectations you are attached to are the caused strain on your relationship.
- You are a stay at home parent and do not contribute revenue. You provide childcare, but we both need to budget better. Something has to give, which means some of the activities and expectations have to be removed so the free time and energy can be better used to focusing on the priorities.
- You and your family are over-scheduled and attached to an outdated vision of a perfect

household that is not easily maintainable by one person doing everything by themselves.
- You are a people pleaser who accepted new commitments even if there is no time and money to do it all.
- You are not able to say no to your children and say no to yourself when you want something that you do not have the time or money to do.
- You have a hard time adapting and changing your expectations that are not working with your lifestyle. This is the cause of your angry outbursts and forceful demeanor to your family that are not seen by others outside the household.

Lack of Correct Thought:
- The person is not thinking out the situation before they start making assumptions about the other person not wanting to participate in their family's daily activities.

- The person is not thinking out the circumstances to why their spouse is constantly tired and has no time to fulfill commitments they have. Plus, the person is not thinking out the circumstances to why they are exhausted trying to meet up with their own unrealistic expectations.

Lack of Correct Speech:
- The person is making inaccurate statements with limited understanding of why their spouse is not able to fulfill commitments.
- The person is cutting off the other person from having a two-way conversation, because they do not want or care to compromise with the person. They will bully the conversation to get what they want at all costs even if it means slowly ruining the bonds of their relationship over time. This person speaks from a narcissistic point of view. This type of personality may stem

from a spoiled childhood where they get whatever they want by learning how to bully others or this is a defense mechanism to hurt others 1st so they don't get hurt back.

- The person is also making statements about themselves that are a reflection of their own failures and not understanding that they need to unload some of the excessive attachments that is causing this poor self-talk. The poor self-talk may be a learned attribute in childhood that they learned from their family.

Lack of Correct Actions:

- You lack discipline to say no to yourself, your kids, and other people who ask you to commit to more activities that you do not have the time or money to afford to do. You need to practice the act of saying, "no thank you". You need to practice the act of instilling boundaries for yourself and knowing when you have reached your limit. Regardless, if you may disappoint others, you need to let go of childhood fears of not being accepted by others that caused you to become a people-pleaser.

- You need to practice the act of setting priorities and letting go of small things that are not a priority. This will allow for more wiggle room to get a part-time job, feel less exhausted, complete school work to train for job advancements, and just accept that you are fine if the house is not spotless, but somewhat clean.
- You need to make it an action point to set time aside every day to spend time with your spouse and family when he/she is home doing family activities or date night activities regardless if you don't spend the time to tackle more of that excessive to-do list that I hope you have slimmed down to

what the real priorities are and stuff that you can live with being marginally ok. You need to let go of that perfect image of yourself and accept you are multi-faceted.

Lack of Correct Livelihood:
- The person is living a lifestyle that does not work with what they want. Based on the income they have to share, the person(s) need to live modestly so that the spouse has time to fulfill personal obligations.
- In order to have the time and energy to focus on the lifestyle where the family is spending more time together, you both have to work to make the money to continue the lifestyle you're living or remove some of the commitments your family is part-taking in. Instead, use the free time to spend together.

Lack of Correct Understanding:
- You have to understand that the need to fulfill all the activities and commitments is due to your inability to say no, your over zealousness to take on more than you can handle, or your lack of insight. The lack of insight is that the core issue behind why you overschedule yourself is that you have a hard time focusing on a few things to excel in it and appreciate it. You need to get other people's praise of you for doing all these things. You need to get your own approval that you can commit to take on more than you can handle.
- The person is looking at one angle and not taking responsibility in their part of what contributes to their spouse constantly working and away. The person does not understand what the other person has to go through for this person to enjoy their lifestyle. On the other side, the working

parent does not understand the work involved in maintaining the household and why their spouse needs a break when he/she gets home from work. Both parents need to sit down and list out all the things they do in the day and start prioritizing what needs to be kept and what they can live without doing.

Lack of Correct Effort:
- If the couple wants to maintain the lifestyle they cannot afford, then both parents need to put the effort into working the jobs that'll provide the income to maintain that lifestyle. They need to make an effort to communicate where they need help and find creative ways to break up the household chores to make it manageable.
- If both spouses practice limiting their commitments both at work and at home to spare their time and energy to be able to

focus that effort on their family commitments, then they need to continue that effort moving forward by not going back to creating a long to-do list of home chores and adding more projects at work that take up more energy outside of what is needed. It's a give and take and they have to prioritize where they will put the effort into. Again you are the cause and these issues you experience are the effect. You need to list out all the things you do and prioritize what you want to focus your effort into. Let go of the things that take up time and money that is not important to you and accept your decision.

Lack of Correct Concentration:
- If the jobs both parents need to have to maintain their lifestyle are something that needs more training and education to qualify for, then they must concentrate on

attaining those requirements. Likely, they will not get jobs they do not qualify for. Be open to putting your concentration on constantly learning and be trainable. You limit your growth if you are not a constant student in life, because economies change. Since economics change and your livelihood is based on your ability to adapt, then you must concentrate on doing the things you need to do to achieve the lifestyle you want.

- You need to concentrate on the list of things you have prioritized and focus on doing them well. If it is a distraction that takes you away from accomplishing your tasks you have prioritized, then concentrate of reverting back to the tasks at hand.

Lack of Correct Mindfulness:

- The couple needs to be aware of the small decisions they make every day that are causing them to live out of their means. Making conscious decisions that relate to reducing the suffering they have is living mindfully.

- They need to be mindful of the economic state they are in and forget about how other people view them. If they have little income and one person has to stay home to take care of young children while the other works, then they both need to be aware of their circumstances. Being mindful of this will allow them to do more with the little resources they have.
- If the spouse cannot work and has little ones at home, but they need a little extra income, then they may consider offering legitimate childcare services in their home to other working parents. Creative problem solving will work if they are conscious of how their problems are created.

Suffering #2:

I don't have the money I need to pay my bills, because I'm constantly changing jobs. I refuse to work an entry level job in the meantime until a job that fits my credentials come up, because I am too good for it. I don't want to work and expect others to pay for me. I procrastinate on looking for a job and just lazy. I rather squat at someone else's expense so I can escape in my addictions than work for my livelihood.

Attachment (s):
- This person is attached to the idea that they're special. They're attached to the perspective that they're better than someone else, which is why they will refuse to work a part-time job or entry level position while looking for a better job. The attachment they have is a notion that they're more qualified and more skilled than the people working an entry-level job

is, which is why they would rather not work and deplete their resources to the point that they run out of money to pay their bills instead of belittling themselves to working an entry level job in the meantime.

- They're attached to the concept of a perfect job for themselves and none of the jobs have met their expectations. So, they jump from one job to another looking for the right fit. The minute they find something or someone that they don't like that doesn't meet their attached expectation of what a job they will stay for comes, then they quit.
- They don't want to work and expect others to pay for them, because they're attached to the expectation that their family is responsible for their welfare and they have to take care of family. They're attached to the concept that family will always bail them out and help them out at all costs.

- They procrastinate on looking for a job, because they're attached to the belief that life is a party. They're attached to the welfare system and there are programs to help pay their bills and their family will pay their bills. They're attached to the belief that they're special and do not need to work.
- They're attached to the belief that their family and friends will always help them. So, they squat at someone else's expense so they can escape in their addictions than work for their livelihood. They're attached to feeling good and nothing else matter.
- They're attached to being depressed for much longer than need be and wallowing in their sorrows so it can be an excuse they use so their family and friends can support them. They will never have to take care of themselves as long as they continue to be needy.

Cause (s):

- The cause to why this type of person does not want to work and stick to their job is because they think they are special. They think they are entitled to have everyone help them, because they are special.
- Their privilege or spoiled upbringing was the cause to raise them to believe that they're special and everything should be given to them without having to work for it.
- Their childhood where everyone in the in their family always looked out for them as the youngest, as the only child, as the only girl or boy in the family, and a number of other cadences they hold are the cause to their attached belief that they're special.

Lack of Correct Thought:

- This person has a limited thought process and refuses to look at their problems in a logical format. The logical approach is if they need money to pay their bills, then they need to get a job. All the other reasoning they have for why they cannot be chosen distractions. If they are physically able to work and have the time to work, then their procrastination from their attachments are factoring to their thought process of being special. Even if they are sick and have circumstances making it hard for them to work and have no one to cover for them, they'll find ways to work anyways.

- The limiting thinking process to be irresponsible is a one-sided concept. People who have one-sided thinking processes are narcissistic and often others leave them as they are used to exhausting others resources to fulfill their needs. This one-sided thinking process is a result of not wanting to see the full picture and understanding all angles of how their suffering was created.

Lack of Correct Speech:

- The words and definitions used in one-sided perspectives are often excuses and complaints. The speech is incorrect in that it is not complete with logic and reasoning.
- People stuck in a one-sided conversation will likely have people stop talking to them as others have realized that you do not have two-way conversations with these types of people. This person refuses to listen to reasoning and solutions to their suffering. This person can only justify their suffering by having a narcissistic speech. This person uses one sided self-talk to convince themselves that they are innocent of their suffering and everyone else who won't enable them by helping them out is contributing to their suffering.

Lack of Correct Actions:
- This person suffers from inaction. They want a healthy lifestyle delivered to them without having to work for it. Their belief that they are special and everyone else will take care of them contributes to their laziness and lack of action towards finding, keeping, and working a job that will provide the income to sustain their lifestyle.

Lack of Correct Livelihood:
- This person does not live the mini action steps they need to solve their dilemma. If they wanted to end their suffering of not having money from not having a job, then they would wake up every day to apply for jobs that meet their skill sets. They would put the steps into getting the training and education they need to qualify for better jobs they desire. They would follow-up with applications they sent out. If they have a

job, then they would work every day with good work ethic to maintain their job. Livelihood is just doing the needed steps throughout your day that contributes to the intended goal to finding and keeping a job to pay their bills.

Lack of Correct Understanding:
- The suffering of this type is caused by the person's refusal to understand the parameters that got them in this situation and refusal to understand the parameters that kept them broke.

Lack of Correct Effort:
- This person lacks the effort that they do not put into fixing their issues. They are not contributing the energy towards doing the things they need to work towards ending their suffering in this situation. This person has given up. Lack of effort is due to lack if

interested in doing the needed work to maintain their lifestyle.

Lack of Correct Concentration:
- In these situations, the person is concentrating on doing nothing to change their situation. The act of no action is also an action that is producing more depravation. This person needs to concentrate on acting on the solutions that will get them out of famine and work towards opportunities to get a job that will provide income to sustain their livelihood.
- This person wants more satisfaction from their job may also be letting other people's perception of their worthiness to be promoted or qualified hold them back from working for what they want. In this situation, this person can do two things. They can work the standard pathway they have found that may or may not be outlined

by their company or they can find alternative pathways that can get the experience they want. They don't need to stop what they are working towards just because one door has been closed to them. They can even be entrepreneurs by creating their own opportunities. I suggest doing research on what other people are doing in their intended field and find small ways to learn some of the skills they need to become qualified in the new interest they want to experience. Over time, that continued concentration will open new opportunities they haven't considered as they will eventually become an expert on their topic of interest and become a resource to others. This is the entrepreneur mindset. For example, if the person wants to become a photographer as a side job, then they can buy a cheap camera that gives them the quality images they want and start taking pictures of their intended audience. They will learn what popular images in that genre are and build a portfolio that amazes potential clients. The experience and the resulting portfolio will make them competitive and allow them to start selling their service to people looking for that type of photography. Client after client testimonials will start piling up on their business website. Before this person knows it, they have become a professional that started a small side business that brings in extra income outside of their primary job. So the continued concentration in what they wanted has now made them even more qualified for their primary job if the skills that they earned from their side job relates to their current primary job. If not, then they opened their own opportunity to do multiple things that make them happy.

Lack of Correct Mindfulness:

- This person is not aware due to limiting themselves from seeing the full picture in how their situation is self-created and sustained or refusing to take responsibility and move forward towards making changes to better their situation. They are choosing not to be mindful of how this transpired and why their inability to let go of this victim state is aggravating more depressed deprivation.

Suffering #3:

I don't have the relationship I want with my kids. I raised my kids and it's their job to spend much of their time to keep me company. My adult kids need to pay for my livelihood. I have a physically and/or emotionally abusive, manipulative, and bigot nature to how I have treated my children, but they still need to have a hallmark relationship with me as adults.

Attachment (s):
- This type of person is attached to the view that they deserve a hallmark relationship regardless of how they treat others or the little time they spent with their children during their childhood years. It doesn't matter how they treated them, but they're attached to the expectation that their children need to love them regardless of their nature and treatment now and in the past because they are their parent.
- They're attached to the expectation that their children need to keep them company and care for their welfare in their senior years, because they raised them and it's their turn. Their expectation is that their children's adult lives need to be in constant contact and involvement with them instead of their adult children using much of their time living their lives.

Cause (s):

- The cause of why this person does not have the relationship they want with their adult kids or currently growing child is due to their absentee parenting style. The rift in this relationship is caused by the parent not supporting their child emotionally and physically by providing regular interaction and engaging in their life.

- The cause to why the parent feels lonely now that their children have grown up and moved onto living their own lives are due to having no one to care for. This person suffers from a lack of value in their purpose. If the person continues to not look for hobbies or other areas that they can be fulfilled with, then they will continue to cause loneliness and neediness and use those empty feelings to try to quilt their adult children to use much of their life and resources not living their lives and instead spending it with their aging parent(s).

- The cause to why this person suffers from a lack of resources in their senior years to care for themselves is due to their part in not planning well for their retirement. They have squandered their working years by not contributing to their retirement plans. They too may have not practiced boundaries with themselves and their loved ones by using their income on frivolous items and paying for other people's livelihood instead of contributing to their nest egg. Now, they are using quilt to try to get their adult children to care for them even if their children may not be able to financially.

Lack of Correct Thought:

- This person has not thought out all the factors that created this situation. If the different aspects of these scenarios were thought through, then they would not suffer and be able to creatively problem solve so they can move forward with creating other more enriching experiences. Moving forward, this person needs to think about how they feel regarding their relationships with their kids and think about how their actions moving forward will affect their relationships.

Lack of Correct Speech:
- The words that this person has spoken to others are ones of quilt that is used to manipulate other's good nature into doing what they want. Harsh words are also commonly used to harm those that they supposedly love. Also, harsh words and down talk are used on themselves to keep them in the victimhood state. This person needs to begin speaking more kind to others and themselves. If this person is no

longer interested in the victimization state, then they are ready to move forward into creative actions that lead to problem-solving.

Lack of Correct Actions:

- As you can see, the lack of actions or the actions that this person has done are what has brought them to this situation. The poor choices in actions toward depleting their resources and also to not allocate their resources appropriately towards their retirement are what have provided such lack in later years. Moving forward, this person needs to outline the mini action steps they are going to do to build a better relationship with others and themselves so they do not repeat the same lessons.

Lack of Correct Livelihood:
- This person has been living a life that contributed to the suffering they endure. Livelihood is the actions that someone takes every moment that builds a lifestyle. This person has created this lifestyle of famine by living a life where their actions were one of squandering their resources instead of saving some of it towards their retirement years. They have spent their time performing hurtful acts and speeches onto their family and themselves to get what they want. They have not worked on creating a good relationship by not participating in their child's upbringing. There are many ways you can diagnose the everyday actions that this person has done that contributed to the end result they are suffering from now. If they want to change their situation, then they need to start living a life full of actions, thoughts, and words

that support the new outcome they want to manifest. They were the cause of the effects they are suffering from. If they want to change the effects, hence their current predicaments, then they need to change the attached expectations that are the root cause of the life they are living.

Lack of Correct Understanding:
- This person needs to understand the feelings that their actions and inactions have caused for those involved in their torn relationship. Refusal to understand what someone has gone through by your actions is a sign of a narcissist who only is interested in a one-sided relationship. Narcissistic persons do not have a fulfilling relationship and only learn from severe pain of driving everyone they know and love away from them through toxic behaviors. If this person refused to try to understand all

perspectives and work on creative problem solving with those understandings in mind, then the way to work with them is to not work with them at all. The act of no options is also an option that can force a narcissist to reflect on their actions and start making positive changes in their life.

Lack of Correct Effort:
- In these situations, the solution to them requires creative problem solving. This person needs to put the effort into repairing any emotional and physical damage they have part take in with their children by addressing the suffering inflicted on their children and asking for forgiveness. My definition of forgiveness is the act of accepting what happened and letting go of the anger you have about it. The anger is the energy that keeps the pattern going and transpiring into repeat

lessons for the child in their life. The hurtful acts happened. Dwelling on it only keeps this person the victim of circumstances. Learning from the experiences will shed light on it and making peace with it. It is accepting it happened and learning from it. If this person learned from it, then they don't need to continue to hold anger towards those hurtful experiences any longer. If the child or parent who was hurt still has anger, then they have not forgiven everyone and themselves for what transpired. If they are ready to move on and change their frequency for a better reality, then they need to accept and let go of the anger they have about the experience. In essence, forgive. It doesn't matter if others forgive them, because they are the cause and everyone else is the effect. So, they must forgive in this situation to free themselves of the energy surrounding this hurtful relationship in order to change their energy signature and co-create with God a better reality for themselves to experience next. In all these scenarios of suffering, the parent or child needs to accept their part in the issues that caused a rift in their relationship that has manifested into their reality and forgive it all. Make the effort to forgive.

Lack of Correct Concentration:

- Knowing the cause of how these sufferings were created, this person needs to concentrate every day on not going back to the habits that caused these issues in the 1st place. When life is starting to be enjoyable again, some people can tend to revert back to their old ways and show they have not learned anything. As such, they re-create in new ways, the same issues until they painfully learn their lessons. If the parent and/or child have learned from these experiences, then they need to continue to focus their thoughts and concentrate on living the actions and holding the positive feelings about their new relationship without holding onto the old baggage of past hurt feelings from old hurtful experiences that they say they have forgiven.

Lack of Correct Mindfulness:
- Moving forward, this person needs to keep in mind how their situations came about and live with knowing how to not repeat the circumstances that put them in such predicaments in the first place. They need to be conscious and aware of their environment, how they think about their relationship, and how they act. Those actions such as guilting their children, saying mean things, and doing manipulative

things show that they have not learned. More torn relationships with their children will be created by them choosing not to be mindful of how their actions produce related outcomes and by not reflecting their new beliefs back into new experiences.

Suffering #4:

I don't have a career I'm proud of. I don't like my job. I want a job I enjoy. I worked to get this job, but now I don't like it.

Attachment (s):

- This person is attached to the view that they deserve a better job even if they don't qualify. They're attached to the view that they're special and people should just give me the job they want even though other people who are a better fit are applying for the same job.

- They're attached to the belief that their job or career should always be something they enjoy. They don't want to recognize that some jobs are stepping stones to get the skills they need for a better job.
- They're attached to the expectation that they should enjoy all aspects of their job every day and that changes in their job do not occur.
- They're attached to the fantasy that this job they worked for is supposed to be something it is not. They did not realize it would end up being something entirely different than what they thought it was going to be like.

Cause (s):
- The cause to why this person does not have a career they are proud of is because every job they take in the same field over time builds into a career path. Looking back at

their work experience is reflecting over their career. This person may have jumped job to job in different disciplines. They did not over time develop a mature career beginning with their first entry level position and working towards their senior level position when they retired from the workforce. The cause to not having a career that was fulfilling is due to their inability to find an area of interest that excited them and apply themselves to working job opportunities in that field from one entry level position to the next level position and onwards until they have completed that career path. By following and advancing in the same field in their career, then they'll have a career that they are proud of when they reflect on it later.

- Some other causes for this dissatisfaction in their career can come from them holding themselves back with their fears by not taking opportunities that were stepping stones up to higher paying, notable jobs in their field of interest. They may have chosen to not go to school and get the education they needed to qualify for the jobs in their career path of interest, because of their fear of the cost of tuition, being tied to staying close by love ones instead of moving on, and so many other fears that keep people held back from reaching their full potential career.

Lack of Correct Thought:
- This person lacks the ability to think out how this situation transpired. If they sat down and listed out all the jobs they had and what experiences they gained from it that qualified them for a better job in the same field or cross-related field, then they will see where the disconnect in their thought process about their current

dissatisfaction comes from. They can see the disjointed thought process that is missing from their analysis.

Lack of Correct Speech:
- This person has been speaking out into existence that they wanted a specific career and acting differently by not doing the steps needed to get into their fantasied career path. More common is that many people do not know what they want in a career that they love to do. They say they want one thing or like a couple things in that career, but do not think about the other aspects of the career that may not be something they want to do. When this person speaks about what they want, they need to be clear in the words they choose. For example, if they want to be a certain professional. Then they have to speak about their desires and interests in that profession. They need to

engage in conversations with people and topics of interests in that profession. They need to not jump around to other careers to speak about and only focus their words on the one area of interest that they are building a career path around.

Lack of Correct Actions:

- Along with aligning their words to fit what career they want; they must put their energy into action. This person has not participated in the action steps they are required to have the jobs and work the career they say they desire. This person has to be consistent and continue to work towards the career they are interested in and will be fulfilled emotionally from. The action this person needs is to seek the skills and training needed to perform the job functions in their desired career. If they need to go back to school to get the degree needed for the job such as a medical degree to be a doctor, then that is the action they need to apply for and complete before the job opportunity can be applied for. If they have the education and need experience working with patients before they can practice with a license in medicine, then the person needs to apply for and complete an internship or hands-on work experience as an understudy. As you can see, these are jobs that have the function of a stepping stone or transitional purpose that the person needs to act on in order to get to do their dream job.

Lack of Correct Livelihood:
- This person is practicing the moment to moment actions of inaction to stay in this perpetuated non-producing state of consciousness. Sitting around and not fulfilling the steps he/she needs to seek,

apply for, and work a job is what is keeping them in this chosen suffering for much longer. The timeframe it takes to find a job may be different from market to market, but not getting up to change their actions will keep them living in this state of financial desperation. If they want to change their livelihood, then they need to start having action in the steps they need to do that working people do.

Lack of Correct Understanding:
- In the case of someone who has achieved a job that they want and realize that it is not something they want; this person lacks the understanding of the reality of the job. They did not do thorough research to see the different aspects of the career before devoting energy into qualifying for it.
- The person also lacks the understanding that the job will change and evolve. As

changes in any career and job will eventually change, the person must adapt to industry changes, company changes, and changes in job responsibility.

- This person could also be lacking the understanding that they may feel they are "special". That they are so special in their family and in a society that they unconsciously expect everyone in their life to rescue to them and bail them out. If their loved ones choose to not come save them, then they blame others for their misfortunes, hold a grudge and dig these situations back up when it suits them in the conversation and hold anger over others for not coming to rescue them from their own self-inflicted suffering.

- This person may lack the understanding that they may have exhausted all of their family's and friend's trust and resources in many past self-created emergency crisis's that the only way for their love ones to help them is to choose to not commiserate with, coddle, and enable this person to continue their bad habits. By deciding not to have anything to do with this person and not help them at all, it forces this person to hit their lowest low. This person has no choice left but to learn to pick themselves up and start taking care of themselves. Otherwise, if this person does not take care of themselves, then it is them who is the cause of their suffering and despair. Those who choose to practice hard love should not feel quilty for doing so as they have exhausted their options trying to help this person out. The only thing left to offer is the last remaining choice, which is to let them fall on their face.

- This person lacks the understanding that their "prolonged" inability to work on providing a livelihood for themselves and quit doing things, because it feels too hard for them to continue to do is an escapism strategy. Escapism is any actions that are jeopardizing to their personal welfare in the form of addictions, toxic behavior, lack of working to care for themselves, and others that avoid taking responsibility for the decisions that affect their livelihood. This is a form of lack of self-respect and self-love. This person lacks the ability to love themselves. They do not care to provide for themselves. If this person cares for themselves and loves themselves instead of using their mommy and/or daddy issues and any other unconscious childhood influences that they have internalized as the contributing factor to their low self-esteem and lack of self-love, then they will put the effort to work on providing an enriching life for themselves.

- If this person realized that they want to work, but gives up often, then they lack understanding that all things in life run in a cycle and patterns. They do not need to know everything and know how to do anything. They just need to apply themselves. They need to be open to learning and commit to the process of learning and working their way up into different job opportunities that are one stepping stone to another stepping stone. Over time, those different related and cross-related jobs have developed them into a highly skilled person in that field of interest. The whole work span is what a career path is.
- Basically, the person needs to analyze the different aspects that factor into their dissatisfaction with their career or job in order to get a clear understanding how it

was created and begin the process of creative problem solving.

Lack of Correct Effort:
- This person has put their effort into continuing to perpetuate their dissatisfaction with their career and job. Continuing to complain about the unwanted job will only grow the despair they feel and make them further hate their job to the point that it becomes debilitating. If this person wants to move beyond this dissatisfaction about their job, then they need to start focusing their effort and energy into seeking out an alternative job that is either closely related to their industry if they are happy with their industry or seek a new career path knowing that they may be starting the journey towards advancement in that new intended field of interest at the entry-level. Where

they put their energy is where their career will grow.

- If they like their job and their career path so far, but the changes in their job tasks or the persons they work with are the changing factors to their prolonged dissatisfaction, then this person should consider putting their energy into seek another cross-related job in the same industry so that they do not have to begin again on a new career path.

Lack of Correct Concentration:

- So far, this person has concentrated on the aspects of their job that they do not like and it has grown to the point that they do not like their overall job or career. If they want to change this, then they need to begin to set their concentration on taking a different perspective about what they liked in their job, which can provide insights that make them happy about their current income source. If the job that they are working in is fine, but their dissatisfaction comes from needing a different industry perspective to appreciate it, then this person may need focused concentration on looking for an alternative career to pursue. Disjointed concentration for small periods of time is jumping around from one interest to another that is not related and cannot be work together. That is not concentrating. That is indecision on what they want. Again, they are the cause and everything else the effect. So, they need to decide what they want to concentrate on and stay focus on the pathway to working on that career by taking job after job that relates to their chosen career path.

Lack of Correct Mindfulness:
- Not feeling satisfaction from your job is a common type of suffering. These people

have to be mindful and self-aware of the things that they do and understand that everything that they think and do creates the effects or outcome that they have worked for. If they have clarity in what they want to do for work, then they need to be mindful of not letting themselves be distracted by other interests and not accept invitations from outside persons that will take them away from the thoughts and actions they are doing to achieve this career goal. If they allow themselves to be distracted and jump around to other interests and do not commit to the things, they need to do to qualify for the opportunities that generate their overall career, then they suffer from confusion and not knowing what they want. They must keep their eye on the prize and be mindful everyday about their goal. Be and do what they need to get that job.

Suffering #5:

I have mommy and/or daddy issues from my toxic childhood. I go from one bad relationship to another. I keep having arguments and fights with my partner. I have commitment issues. I latch onto everybody I am with and I am exhausting to them. I am repeating the same toxic relationship of my parents, but I don't know how to be any different.

Attachment (s):
- This person is attached to justifying their hurt. Therefore, they will not forgive, let go of the anger, and hold a grudge so that they can unconsciously sabotage themselves for not feeling adequate and loved in childhood.
- This person may also be attached to the view that they can rescue, change, or be someone's hero in order to validate themselves. They may believe that they do

not deserve a healthy relationship free of drama or that they don't know what healthy is. They may only know drama and are repeating pre-existing conditioning from my childhood. Their attachment to their unconscious view that they're not worthy of a healthy relationship from what they learned in childhood watching their parents fight and live in hatred of their poor relationship could be an unconscious expectation that they held about what a marriage and relationship is supposed to be like.

- They may treat their children with hurtful words and actions, because they're attached to an unconscious belief that children need to be punished in order to raise them like they were raised. They may be unconsciously exercising the teachings of their upbringing from their parents who showed them how to be a parent. They may be unaware of their unconscious attachment to this style of parenting even though they did not like the effects it had on them as a child and do not like the effects that the passed down parenting style has on their own children. They may not know that they do not know how to be a better parent than what I have been taught.

- They start fights with their family and partner when things are peaceful and working out, because they're attached to the perspective that they are not worthy of a healthy relationship and family. This may be due to their unconscious belief in their upbringing that has taught them how to live with a tormented, abusive childhood that their parent(s) may have inflicted on them that they are either unconsciously repeating or using as an outlet to relieve stress.

- They may also have commitment issues, because they are attached to an unconscious belief that they have about living in fear of making a mistake and reliving their parent's toxic relationship. Their commitment issues could also be due to the attachment to a belief that they are expected to not fail due to the high expectations others have placed on them. They may also be attached to a belief that they need a lot of information to be confident in their decision to commit.

Cause (s):
- Their parent(s) were not great to them. Since their parent(s) were not good to them and they were raised in a toxic and abusive household, they may self-sabotage their own happiness in an unconscious effort to punish themselves and continue to live in a harmful relationship like the one that they

were raised in. They may have accepted the idea that this is the kind of relationship that they learned from their parents marrital example and as such, they must deserve this relationship style. They are not recognizing the patterns in their decision to attract an abusive relationship or be the abuser in the relationship only continues to unconsciously repeat the same familial pattern, which is the cause of this person's suffering. They are just repeating learned conditioning from their upbringing. Analyzing and recognizing this is the 1st step to deciding if they want to continue to live in this toxic manner in their relationships or learn new patterns for living peacefully in their relationships.

- The cause for people who seek destructive and narcissist people to have a relationship with can arise from an unconscious search for fulfillment and approval through people who inflict pain onto them. These people can be unconsciously tied a childhood where they were emotionally and possibly physically abused and at times neglected by a narcissist parent(s) themselves. In an effort to seek out the affection of someone like their parent(s), they repeatedly find themselves attracting people who like their abusive parent(s) look for caretaker individuals who need approval and control from a narcissistic personality. The cause is that the adult child still wants to be accepted and loved by their parent(s). This person may be playing out a repeated cycle of destructive relationships in order to get the lost affection they desire from their parents in childhood. The cause could also stem from not being able to accept the nature of their relationship with their parents and so they continue to seek a hallmark fantasy relationship with their estranged parent(s) trying much of their lives to make a worth parent-child relationship out of a damaging childhood. This person continues to cause themselves suffering by refusing to accept the character defect and flawed demeanor of their narcissi, one-sided parent(s) and let go of the anger they hold about not having the loving childhood they continue to seek in repeating such relationships in their adult lives.

- The people I have found that latch onto everybody they are with and are exhausting to them. This may be caused by their unknown childhood fear of rejection and abandonment. Their childhood may have been one of devastation and lack a loving household, so this person finds people who have a hero complex and finds fulfillment in saving emotionally unstable people. These types of situations are also caused by the person who happens to constantly be in crisis and finds people to help them. By not having the self-love and self-respect to care for their own livelihood, this person continues to make poor choices to self-sabotage their own successes so that they do not have to learn to care for themselves and instead have crisis's situations that use other people's energy, time, and resources to help them in their lives. These self-inflicted causes will take so much time away from other people's lives that those who constantly help them have little time to manage their own life, their own relationships, and become the beck and call to these "victim narcissi" that use them. When there are no longer resources to use others, these "victim, and one-sided narcissists" will move on to find new people to help them.

- In simple terms, people who suffer from mommy and/or daddy issues cause their perpetual suffering by not accepting their childhood was what it was and they need to let go of the anger surrounding it. Otherwise, not realizing their repeat patterns of abusive relationships is choosing to continue to punish themselves through their childhood traumas. It's an endless cycle of running for approval and never getting it, because the lesson was to learn that you are the one in control of your livelihood now. Learn from it and learn new ways to care for themselves by learning what a healthy relationship is like and how to maintain such relationships full of peace instead of constant newly created dramas. These dramatic fights are often self-created and a call from a child unconsciously looking for love and affection that they did not have growing up.

Lack of Correct Thought:
- This person is so caught up in the day to day activities of dealing with toxic relationships that they lack the time to stop and think about the causes that they are holding onto that cause them to continue living out the thought patterns of abuse and neglect. It drives their need to sustain such relationships. When this person analyzes their afflictions in their crisis relationships, then they can choose to either stay in the cycle of abuse that they inflict onto others or suffer from abuse onto themselves and leave the abusive relationship style they unconsciously are attracted to.

Lack of Correct Speech:
- This person lacks self-love and it comes in their speech.
- Many times, and in many different ways, the mommy and/or daddy issues this

person suffers from will crop up in the words and in the way that they communicate to themselves and to others. They can choose harmful bad talk to others as a way to wound others before they are wounded, which is a defense mechanism. They will also at times, speak poorly about themselves and not give themselves much credit. These types of poor speech will be an unconscious way of keeping them in the cycle of deprived abuse. If they recognize this and want to change for the better, then they need to start being more aware of how they speak to others and how they speak about themselves to themselves.

- Another style of poor self-talk is to shut down and not talk at all about their issues and to not communicate to others. This form of bad non-verbal talk is an escapist strategy to not uncover the underlying causes to their issues so that it does not get resolved and does not force them to learn new, healthier ways to communicate with people. I find these people will cut the conversation off so that they don't have to address the issues and have a two-way conversation to uncover the pain and resolve the issues that they may be part of creating or perpetuating.

Lack of Correct Actions:
- This person lacks the actions of what a healthy relationship looks like. Instead of appreciating the peace and calm as a sign of serenity in a loving relationship like a comforting blanket, this person will plan and seek opportunities for discourse that will play out in a major drama. Their toxic, damaging actions have been bent on doing things that are hurtful to others and to themselves by thinking only of their gain though finding ways to be the victim in the

situation. If this person wants to be in a healthy relationship, then they need to learn new ways of being and behaving. Those types of action steps they do are what they are lacking. Noticing their poor behavior in different day-to-day mini actions will help to the address that, stop it, and replace those damaging actions with actions that are more peaceful and fulfilling.

Lack of Correct Livelihood:
- The livelihood that is missing are those mini actions they live with every day. All those non-dramatic actions are what make a complete livelihood. The person has to be content with living in peace, harmony, and joy without needing to create a crisis to feel victim in and get healing attention from. Living in constant crisis is draining to both parties. Eventually, someone gets tired of it and will move on. In other words, if this

person does not recognize the mini actions, they take every day, then they will continue to re-create more and more crisis situations in relationship after relationship.

Lack of Correct Understanding:
- This person may lack the understanding of why they are unaware of repeating bad learned behaviors that are manifesting in their toxic relationships. They need to step aside from their situation and look at how their childhood was like and see if it is a reflection of what they learned from their parents who are their closest example of what a relationship looks like. Once they see the repeating destructive patterns as either the perpetrator or the victim, then they can decide if it is beneficial for them to continue in this manner or seek new ways to behave in a relationship. Eventually, that

learned conditioning is the understanding they lack and may be seeking.

Lack of Correct Effort:
- This person has put a lot of energy and emotions into sustaining a toxic relationship as either the dominate controller or the weak victim. They have to decide if they want more of the same abusive style of relationships in a companionship or friendships as it will worsen to the point of becoming life threatening to someone. If they have children, then they may subject their children to endure watching how to be in an abusive relationship. Their effort is put into the abusive style and they need to learn to redirect their energy into putting emphasis into practicing a healthier style of communication and manner of being to others. Where ever they focus their effort that is the path that will grow.

Lack of Correct Concentration:

- The person in these situations may have suffered from a lack of concentration in learning and being in a state of harmony and accepting peace as an acceptable state of being. They may have been on auto-pilot and running through the motions of being in an abusive relationship as the victim who is not worthy and in constant seeking of approval and love or as the abuser who violently controls out of an unconscious state of fear of potential abandonment and rejection. This person needs to address their issues they have about how they see themselves in relation to the childhood they had that perpetuated and instilled that unaware conditioning. By recognizing it, they need to learn to concentrate their time and energy into creating a life full of seeking and maintaining healthy relationships in their romantic life, in their friendships, in their familial relationships, and in their many other relationships. In terms of many other relationships, that can be your destructive relationship you have with money, with your health, with your pets, with how you relate to your spirituality and many more I have not listed that these unknown mommy and daddy issues can bleed into. These are my observations. I'm sure many more can be discovered on a case by case basis.

Lack of Correct Mindfulness:

- The lack of mindfulness regarding mommy and daddy issues that surface into repeating cycles of abusive relationships into adulthood and if not recognized and stopped can grow into the next generation is from a lack of being aware of the conditioning they unconsciously accepted as normal ways of being and behaving.

Once people who suffered from mommy and daddy issues stop and recognize it, then they can decide to stop the cycle of abuse and learn new ways to be. Learning new ways to interact with others in a healthy and peaceful manner is being self-aware of how you were and conducting yourself with kindness and kindness to others by not acting in the destructive mannerisms listed above. That is being mindful of your mommy and daddy issues you no longer choose to exploit and punish yourself with. That courageous recognition of the unconscious beliefs about yourself from your childhood is an act in breaking the cycle of destructive relationships.

Suffering #6:
> I don't like my body and I am over weight.

Attachment (s):
- This person may be attached to the weigh as a protective armor to prevent addressing the issues that caused the weight gain.

Cause (s):
- This person may have a bad diet and don't exercise.
- This person may also have bad knees, joints, or a variety of other issues that may make them feel pain if they were to exercise, which is why this person should begin an active lifestyle and exercise regimen slowly that works with their physical ailment and doctor's recommendation.

Lack of Correct Thought:

- The person dealing with the weight issue may lack thinking about the core issues preventing them from living an active lifestyle.

Lack of Correct Speech:

- This person lacks the words needed to reinforce what they want. They may want to be healthy, but ask for junk food or say things like, "I'm tired", "I don't want to exercise", and "I don't have time to exercise." These examples are the kind of speech that this person is using to fuel their body image suffering. They need to start changing how they talk to others and to themselves. Their negative self-talk about their poor body image is just fueling the depressed state of affairs and not motivating them. For some people, poor self-talk can motivate them to do something about it, but for many, it just keeps them down. To change this person's suffering, they need to change their self-talk.

Lack of Correct Actions:
- This person needs to have a healthy process to discover what kind of action they must do to attain and maintain a healthy body. This person may speak about wanting a healthy body, but is not getting off the sofa to take a walk or exercise. If they truly want to be in shape, then they need to start putting their body in action. Otherwise, they do not want to be healthy.

Lack of Correct Livelihood:
- This person lacks the mini action steps that make up their livelihood. They are contributing to their poor fitness by doing actions such as inactivity, stress eating,

binge eating, making themselves feel worst by saying negative things to themselves about their weight, and so many other mini actions that continue to fuel the weight gain and image issues. In order to fix their suffering, this person needs to start taking mini action steps that lead to a healthy and active livelihood. Some examples are waking up praising themselves for being alive and having the ability to change their circumstances. They are the cause and the weight is the effect they created. This person can choose to eat fewer portions and eat more healthy foods. They can drink more water. They can take a walk after meals. They can even buy a cheap exercise bike from the classified ads to put in their living room and get on the bike for 30 minutes every day while watching their favorite TV show or playing video games. You name it. There are many mini action steps that this person can be doing to change their suffering for the better. All those changes are the livelihood that this person must do in order to change their circumstances.

Lack of Correct Understanding:
- This person is refusing to see how they are perpetuating their suffering or just need some education on how to live a healthier lifestyle. They may be refusing to understand that their excuses for why they cannot make time to work out even if they put a cheap exercise bike in their living room next to the TV is their blatant refusal to accept that they are in their state of poor health, because of their laziness. Their laziness that can be a prolonged cause stems from their lack of understanding that if they do not take control of their life choices and be self-responsible for their

welfare in all cases and in this one relating to their health, then they lack self-love. Someone who loves themselves will care for themselves. They may not know how, but they will at least try. The universe will help those who try to be self-responsible.

Lack of Correct Effort:
- It's obvious that this person lacks effort. They are choosing not to exert any energy into acting on their need to exercise and be action in their everyday activities in order to become healthy. Where the energy goes, the results will show. When no energy goes, nothing shows but more of the same. In this case, more weight gain.

Lack of Correct Concentration:
- Concentration is continuing the focused energy to put their energy into the actions they need to do in order to live that healthy

lifestyle. This person needs to continue that momentum and not quit after a couple tries at working out. Fulfilling the Eightfold Path to address this form of body image suffering requires them to continue living with the passion for staying on the active path. If they stop being motivated to work out and make healthy choices, then they are choosing to neglect themselves. Aside from medical issues that can cause weight gain and make it harder to work out, they can still live an active lifestyle and there are many exercise programs catered to many ailments that are adjusted to not cause harm and provide the activity the person needs.

Lack of Correct Mindfulness:
- This person needs to keep in mind the reasons why they started to let themselves go and keep in mind the things they need to

do to stay active and healthy. Insanity is repeating the same things over and over again, but expects a new outcome. So be mindful of the path they choose to walk with regards to their health.

Suffering #7:
Everything would be fine if everyone converted to my religion, politics, culture, etc.

Attachment (s):
- This person is attached to the view that they can rescue, change, or be a hero, because that will validate them.
- They're attached to being right (eous), have a limited view and don't want to see other views in order to stay in their delusion, and/or underestimate that divine consciousness is in all living things unbiased.

Cause (s):

- It's worked for them or hasn't worked for them. Yet, they do it anyways due to conditioning. Inherited conditioning from someone's upbringing is a common cause for this type of segmented, fear-based belief of being self-righteous. The person may not even believe in the concepts taught to them by their parents and cultural upbringing, but they accept it as the truth even though life experiences have proven some of their beliefs to be incorrect. A common conditioning in the west is to believe that they are a result of original sin and for the rest of their life they need to repent of the things someone else prior to them did in their life. As a result, there is an unconscious belief that some people carry around that manifest in their relationships with others and themselves that they are never going to be good enough. They may believe that they will have to spend their whole life paying restitution for the suffering of previous generations in their belief. This conditioning to not practice discernment in passed down belief systems that do not adapt to changes in society and are not universal to all life can cause fanaticism and radicalize someone against others that are not in support of their separatist beliefs. This person may also have a belief in an angry and punishing God, who needs validating from believers and only accepting of certain peoples who belong to their religion or culture. This suffering is caused by the person's need to feel special. This person may think that by belonging to a certain religion and not others and not accepting of others as different formed experiences where souls can learn and grow spiritually from are what makes them special to God. The need to feel accepted and special is the cause of this type of suffering. This person's refusal to see a God that loves all people no matter the circumstances and that consciousness is more accepting, not prejudicial, and separatist as they want it to be so that they can get self-love through being special and chosen. This could be the cause of their suffering. Basically, this person lacks self-love by unconsciously hating others with the beliefs that others not in their faith will not be accepted in the afterlife. Some fanatics of this conditioned belief system that they inherited or converted into could even think that they are doing favors to God by destroying others not in their sect either physically or verbally due to their belief that God needs validating.

Lack of Correct Thought:

- This person lacks thought in asking questions about why they believe what they do and as such act out those beliefs in how they interact and see other people that are not in their religion. This person may be only thinking about spirituality in a limited perspective by only taking into account that life begins at birth or conception and ends in their one lifetime. They may not have thought about what happens to the soul before concept and where did it come from. They may not have thought to themselves, where do all those people who are not "saved" in their terms and conditioned beliefs go to after they die. If it is the underworld they go to, then why would most of the world not in their belief system go there? They may not have thought about the concept of reincarnation that has been written in the textbooks of many of the world's religions or refuses to address those parts of their religious books as it may destroy their belief that they only exist in one lifetime. This segmented belief that supports one lifetime may root from not taking into consideration the effects that the actions they do in this lifetime has for future generations and what factors contributed to the preplanning of the lifetime that they live in now. The belief that all the circumstances that make up their life may be an accident upon conception may be an easy way to coast through life and check out of the karma this person may have that are unresolved in previous lifetimes as they may be creating new karma for their next lifetime. Coasting through life and not learning the painful lessons only keeps this soul on the wheel of karma and preventing them from gaining access to higher level life experiences that the universal library has archived. If this soul cannot accept others and respect others as they are, then no matter how much they love "Star Trek", they will not qualify to incarnate into a galactic society. They have not met the prerequisites for those next level games. They may have not thought about why they believe in the need to appease an angry God by removing the world of people not in their religion and that such damaging actions and damaging talk to others in this manner of unacceptance is needed. They may not think about why they have such a limited belief in God and the reasons why they believe God is angry, judgmental, punishing, separatist, not forgiving, and all the many ways people inflict their man-made belief in being special by creating spiritual barriers to others.

Lack of Correct Speech:
- This person's lack of thinking out the gaps in their belief systems often will also come out in their lack of correct speech. They will say things to other and themselves that make them feel special in regard to their separatist religion. By continuing to speak harshly in religious terms to others and to themselves, then they are perpetuating their limited view on life and the afterlife. Those limitations they repeat to themselves will keep them in a stunted state of consciousness where they do not grow in spiritualty. In Buddhism, your aura and wisdom is a reflection of your spiritual growth. Limiting beliefs about yourself and others are seen as a chosen decision to not grow beyond concepts that are comfortable to them. People who have a highly radiating aura, welcoming persona, wisdom in their being and livelihood, and 6th senses are

those who continue to learn from their mistakes and learn to not create barriers to their spiritual growth. In our society, many people speak into their existing fear based conditioned beliefs from whatever religion they have that create barriers as early on as childhood.

Lack of Correct Actions:

- This person has acted upon the premise that only those in their sect are worthy of their interactions. This person lacks the actions of inclusivity to others who are not like them due to their self-imposed belief that others not belonging to their religious belief are deemed as 2nd class citizens and do not belong to their version of an afterlife, which has caused them to reject taking action such as speaking to and behaving inclusively to others not in their sect. Their lack of inclusive action in small everyday acts prevents them from learning and growing spiritually. They may be religious, but spritualty is an entirely different path and a continual journey. Their religious belief could bring them into a spiritual journey as many roads lead there, but they may need to revise some of their limiting beliefs that could set barriers for their spiritual growth.

Lack of Correct Livelihood:

- All the actions and separated fear-based beliefs that this person has make up their livelihood. If they enjoy living in their perspective, then that is fine. It is when they start pushing their beliefs using fear tactics such as if you do not convert to the way they view entry into the afterlife, the lifestyle they live, their fear-based belief in a hell and a devil that they perpetuate and use to control themselves and others into being subservient to their idolatry, then they can begin to get pushback from others. Not all people who are not part of their religion will want to convert. As a result of rejection from converting to their religion, they either blasphemies others by demonizing them as inferior and will end up in their believed hell and punished for eternity by their believed Satan to make themselves feel special and chosen. This allows them to continue to live in their separatist belief system. They will use it as an excuse to inflict emotional or physical harm onto others by using their beliefs to justify their actions and livelihood. This may be due to them believing that they are doing something for their perceived view of a separatist, vengeful God that needs people to believe in him as they have a limiting view of universal consciousness.

Lack of Correct Understanding:

- This person lacks the understanding that many of the world religions are teaching much of the same core principles through many different teachers that have reached enlightenment and become conscious in the matrix. This person also lacks the understanding that man only knows very little in one lifetime to make judgments on how the afterlife and the universe functions. Instead of keeping an open mind and allowing others to find enlightenment and awakening in their own ways, they are limiting their spiritual growth by holding separatist viewpoints held in the belief that their religion is the only way to be enlightened. If this person comes across 1st hand testimonials that other people in other religions and beliefs had regarding near death experiences and their accounts of how their awakened consciousness changed their reality, then they will need to acknowledge such accounts. Thus, they have chosen to stunt their spiritual growth and soul advancement to stay in their delusion through denial. There will come a point in this person's life that they come across someone that they have come to love that does not confirm to their belief system. They will either be pained by that rejection or learn to accept their loved one as they are and thus accept others as they are all equal reflections of the divine that created them and all other people. They will grow a little more spiritually through accepting others as they are without deeming negatively and learning to let go of their once perceived fear-based and separatist beliefs in order to live more peacefully amongst a diverse landscape of people, cultures, and belief systems. This act of acceptance will widen their belief in a loving and accept version of God and respect for all versions of people created in the universe and truly practice faith in understanding that divine consciousness comes in many forms and spirituality comes in many forms as well.

Lack of Correct Effort:
- The effort this person has lived with is perpetuating their belief system and working on pushing those separatist beliefs onto others. Some people may invite conversion and others do not. This person lacks the understanding that their effort to systematize their one version belief system is fueling a collective consciousness of many people believing in it. At some point that separatist belief will come to a head against people who do not want to convert and that will create a clash. The clashing will show this person that they have a

conditioned belief system that demonizes others not like them and result in negative beliefs of others not being worthy of an all accepting salvation or become the underlying foundation for religious wars that show physically the clash such beliefs how.

Lack of Correct Concentration:

- The continued effort into perpetuating this belief system is fueled by continuing to concentrate on their one version of how people should be even if they, themselves are not living under such moral guidelines they study. Life will eventually contradict their belief by coming across good people who they feel guilty about with their belief that these people will go to hell and choose to go to hell by not converting. They could feel that this is not a fair assessment. The sentiment will force them to concentrate their beliefs on a more accepting version of heaven, of God or it will continue to eat at them. The only way they can continue to concentrate on this separatist version of enlightenment is to only surround themselves by their church members and not the rest of society that refuses to change their upbringing and beliefs as this person is doing the same thing.

Lack of Correct Mindfulness:
- For this person to continue to live the rest of their life in this one version of salvation, this person must choose to not be mindful of other people's differences and that God may not be as separatist and fearful as this person believes God to be. If they want to change, which is usually from coming across someone they have fallen in love with in some type of relationship such as a love for a good friend, a newly married in-law, or

even grandchildren that came from a non-religious, but spiritual parents, then they are forcing themselves to learn to be mindful and aware of the feelings of others when they speak of their separatist beliefs that do not include their new love ones. It is these new found loves that has eased their concerns of a damning and not open salvation and educated them into a more open belief system that accepts all unconditionally as children learning lessons about enlightenment.

Suffering #8:

I'm going through a mid-life crisis. I'm bored. I have the extravagant lifestyle, but I'm not fulfilled. I had a good upbringing with loving parent(s), but I seek instability.

Attachment (s):
- These people are attached to the belief that they are not worthy of such good fortune. They may feel guilty for their blessings and choose to squander it to be less fortunate in order to fit in with others who suffer such lack of fortune.

Cause (s):
- The cause of dissatisfaction for the person who is going through a mid-life crisis and decides to be reckless is due to a loss of purpose once they have reached the end of a journey. They do not know what new passions or purpose they want to work towards now in their later years. This is the same cause for people who are bored and start drama in their life when there was none.
- The cause for a person who had a good upbringing with loving parent(s), but they

seek instability is due to feeling of lack of self-worth. Instead of being thankful that they did something good in past incarnations to be born into a fortunate lifestyle with kind parents and can use that platform to create a life for themselves of success, philanthropy, and maybe even build new things that create wonder to others, they squander their resources. Their destructive decisions are a way to punish themselves for not being less fortunate to mirror how they want to feel inside.

Lack of Correct Thought:
- This person suffers from not thinking out the reasons why they feel the way they do. He or she needs to consider what aspects of their life they are not happy with at this age in their life. If they are suffering a mid-life crisis, then it may be related to not thinking about why they are bored. Their boredom

may relate to a lost in finding ventures and activities that motivate them and make them enjoy their life where it is currently. If they are not fulfilled their lifestyle of comfort and possibly suffering from feeling bad for having a good upbringing, then they need to think about what areas of their feelings that relate to those unfilled thoughts.

Lack of Correct Speech:
- This person has been perpetuating their feelings of ineptness by talking about their dissatisfaction. If they want to change how they feel, then they need to start saying things to themselves that fuel their desire to find purpose and zeal for new creations and activities that excite them and make life fun again. In the case of a person who is feeling guilty for having a good lifestyle and upbringing, then they need to change their

self-talk about not feeling worthy of such blessings.

Lack of Correct Actions:
- This person needs to begin changing the actions they do every day. They may be in this situation by letting life coast by them. If they want to start feeling gratitude and appreciation for their life, then they need to start finding interests and hobbies that excite them. For the person going through a mid-life crisis, they need to start evaluating what action they have done that has produced the outcome they are not happy with. If there is nothing wrong with their relationship or spouse, but they are bored, then replacing their spouse is only a temporary fix that will produce the same type of relationship down the road. This person needs to do a deep live into what aspects of their spousal relationship they

are unhappy with at this age. Their lack of actions in the relationship that they are dissatisfied with can be remedied by introducing new hobbies and activities to spice up their relationship and bring new life to an aged relationship that may suffer the motions of everyday life.

- For the person who is bored, they need to start introducing actions that engage their interests and fascinate them. Finding new interests and activities will produce the actions they need to feel engaged with life again.

- For the person who is unfulfilled by their comfortable lifestyle and for the one seeking instability that was not received by their good upbringing, they need to stop pitying themselves and feeling guilty for not having the hard knocks that other people had to suffer through. They need to be grateful for their blessings and use it as a platform to create new experiences and actions that will benefit other people that they empathize with. By creating projects and volunteering in activities that excite them by helping others, they will appreciate their fortunate circumstances through the help they can give others. Thus allowing them to see and appreciate the good upbringing and lifestyle they were born into instead of taking it for granted and squandering it.

Lack of Correct Livelihood:
- In all these scenarios, these people need to change the day to day activities and beliefs they have that have kept them in such dissatisfaction. Changing the actions they do every day changes the life they live for the better.

Lack of Correct Understanding:

- These different situations require the person to try to understand other people's perspective about their dissatisfaction. They need to understand the circumstances that lead to their dissatisfaction. They also need to look at other people who are involved in their life that directly contribute to their situation. Regarding the person going through a mid-life crisis, he or she needs to understand that the person having the crisis is them and not the other person in the marriage. They may have ended a career and retired and need to find fulfillment in achieving a new career instead of looking at their spouse to fulfill them. They may need to re-evaluate their spouse and see where they have fallen short by letting the relationship grow stagnant and boring. They need to understand that if they want an enriching relationship in their senior years, then they need to find interests and hobbies that excite them and that their spouse may support them in doing. This person lacks the understanding that people are not meant to be stagnant. People are meant to grow and create. By doing so, they will find meaning in their life's work and new works. The same goes for those who lack meaning in their life as that has resulted in boredom and in them being destructive of their good fortunes.

Lack of Correct Effort:
- This person who has achieved success and is born into a comfortable lifestyle need to start putting their effort into using it as a platform to create new experiences of wonder from. They can put their energy into creating a new career that involves their hobby and love of art or music. They can put their effort into using their wealth

and networks into creating or volunteering for activities that provide them gratification through helping others. There is a wealth of ways they can use their platform to be a part of something that creates joy for others and themselves and becomes entrepreneur about their own hobbies. Instead of using their energy to squander their resources, they can use their energy to jump from it and create so much good experiences for themselves. The possibilities are endless.

Lack of Correct Concentration:
- These people need to start concentrating on the positive ways they can use their knowledge, skills, and resources to create magical experiences to be part of.

Lack of Correct Mindfulness:

- Knowing that these people are basically bored and potentially able to create havoc and drama in their life by squandering what they have, and then they need to realize it and stop their own suffering. Moving forward, these people need to keep in mind that they are fortunate to be in the position they are in and use it to create awesome experiences for themselves and others. Basically, stop feeling bored and guilty for having more than others and start using it to benefit others and themselves. Be creative. Start a new venture. Start a new hobby. Learn new artistic skills. There's so much they can do. So, start exploring life again and the people involved in these people lives will become supportive if they start getting excited about life again instead of complaining about how bored they are.

Conclusion

"I am not the first Buddha who came upon Earth, nor shall I be the last."
                    -Siddhartha Gautama

As you may have noticed at the beginning of each chapter, I lead in with a quote from the founder of Buddhism, Siddhartha Gautama. Siddhartha tested out principles he observed in himself and others. He documented his research in the teachings of the Four Noble Truths and

Eightfold Path. These teachings are also documented in visual aids in esoteric artwork about parallel realities and human auras, which to me shows that this knowledge was discovered by many teachers of the very distant past and present that is preserved in art.

As a lover of art though-out my whole life, I study esoteric artwork from indigenous civilizations that date even farther back than when Buddhism was documented as created in 500 B.C.E. In Siddhartha's time, literacy and education were available to the wealthy or monks in monasteries. Many people would enter their children into the monasteries for a free education. As more and more students of Buddhism became teachers, more documents from their 1st hand experience and knowledge got added to the legacy of Buddhism.

These are the foundations of what has over time become the philosophy behind Buddhism. Different cultures and different people have studied it and interpreted the teachings to fit their lifestyle and cultures. Now, there are many different sects of Buddhism that exist today around the world. Some cultures have incorporated their own cultural preferences to hold esteem for men over women in Buddhism among over things, which to me show that the ego of the person still needs to be addressed. No matter the different versions and cultures that adapt the basic principles to accompany their existing belief systems, what remains is the core Four Noble Truths and Eightfold Path.

    Regardless if the student is studying the principles for the 1st time or an experienced practitioner of the principles, the manifesting of parallel realities that is part of their everyday journey in living it is directed by the choices the person makes and not the opinions that others have about their level of enlightenment and ability to work with the energy of the matrix. It is believed by many Buddhists that your soul's spiritual level of advancement is based on your consciousness and the frequency of the human aura that you vibrate at. That vibration radiates two auras, which are the one above your head and the one around your body.

Everyone has a halo and a human energy field. The only difference is the frequency in which it vibrates at, which is subject to the emotions it sends out based on the person's choices that manifest the matching reality he or she lives in. As I have said in the introduction, if you get anything out of this book, it is that you are the cause and everything exterior is the effect. You will only experience the effect that you the cause radiate at. That is the simple explanation of the popular image of many Buddha's with halos and a circular mandala around the person that you see in many Buddhist artworks.

Buddha is a term used to describe a person who is enlightened or basically someone who has awakened to be conscious of their reality and how they manifest within it. It is believed that people are born into their human experience with a veil of forgetting the knowledge they have about the spirit world and the factors that relate to their chosen incarnation so that they can learn and grow from experiencing it firsthand. It is every Buddhist's journey to awaken the Buddha within them. I believe similar artwork from much older civilizations depict the same interpretation I hold.

    For me, my journey began since I was a baby. I was born into the Buddhist philosophy through my Laotian parents who raised me with the principles as best as they could. They are far from perfect and often have their own issues to work through in their lifetime. Growing up in America as political asylums, my parents did their best to try to embrace cultural assimilation, but respect the different faiths of people in America. They tried their best to raise Buddhist children while having missionaries from many faiths try to convert them through making connections with their children through trying to help their kids. Missionaries are a concept that is unique to my parents.

In Laos, it is illegal to give religious materials to people if they did not seek it from you. The airport provide materials to travelers who tour Laos that it is not allowed to disseminate religious pamphlets to local civilians due to a cultural request to respect the heritage of the people and respect their belief in Buddhism unless people directly ask for such materials. Such religious contraband will be confiscated if a missionary is found handing them out to people without permission.

All people are welcome, but be respectful of everyone's incarnations. If they achieved anything from immigrating to America with the wide range of faith systems, it is that they instilled in me that people should accept you as you are and by not accepting your heritage as it is, then they are not able to practice "acceptance", which is the core of other people's suffering. If I understood "acceptance" and "letting go", then I would be much more successful than they have been regarding using the principles in Buddhism to manifest the life I want to live now, rather than wait for the next lifetime to live again in another cycle of reincarnation. My parents are life learners of letting go of the anger they hold for how things transpired and not accepting things happened as they did, good or bad, learn from them, and move forward is a lesson they continue to relearn in so many different ways.

    With the best intentions, my parents always wanted my siblings and I to eventually become self-aware and conscious like the Buddhist artwork that adorns the temples we attended growing up in Seattle, WA. Ultimately, they wanted us to manifest a wonderful life for ourselves and advance so that we qualify to choose out of the many libraries of existences that we could only barely imagine when we choose to reincarnate again the next time.

As a child, I ran around the monastery during temple looking at the pictures of enlightened Buddha's of all forms with their halos and Meta circles depicted around their bodies. I enjoyed the artwork at these monasteries of male Buddha's and especially the famous Chinese female Buddha, Kwan Yin. Literacy is still a skill not often learned by many Buddhist practitioners in many 3rd world countries and artwork is often used throughout the ages to show people the teachings of Buddhism to the poor and illiterate. I hope the literacy rate in 3rd world countries worldwide changes for the better.

I often thought about the artworks of Buddha's who had parallel realities depicted of them rippling out into the ethers and wondered about the images of reincarnation. No one at temple could really explain the images to me beside be good and maybe someday you will learn first-hand what those images you see in many Buddhist monasteries are talking about. I watched so many people come every weekend to temple to pay their respects and get blessings from the monk's chants and dosing of holy water they chanted on the water that is supposed to make the water resonate at a higher frequency to help them make better their lives.

Yet, no matter how many times they attended service and read the materials, I still saw people continue to repeat the same hard lessons over and over again like they never really paid attention to what was discussed in the lectures or like creatures of habit, never truly applied the principles in their own lives. I listened, but dismissed much of the teachings until I can substantiate the philosophy for myself as Siddhartha Gautama often explained. Siddhartha Gautama is renowned for asking his equal practitioners to test out the principles for themselves and don't rely on faith alone. Buddhism is not a religion. It is a philosophy.

Finally, in my late 20's I began to take a closer look at the Buddhist philosophy and apply the principles more actively. The evidence from Consciousness Studies and Quantum Physics started to pour out into the mainstream and it triggered my memories of my Buddhist childhood. I started to research profound metaphysical evidence that the 14th Dalai Lama, Lhamo Dondrub was supporting through his lectures and actively following the works of many esteemed Quantum Physicists and brain researchers all over the world. The new research done by many universities into the nature of reality through Consciousness Studies caught my interest.

As an information junkie, I read whatever I could on the field and listened to all the materials I found from various Buddhist teachers online in order to compare my understanding from my lifetime of living in a Buddhist household to the new scientific research in Quantum Physics and Consciousness Studies or whatever I term the modern title for metaphysical studies is. Now the artworks I pondered about growing up started to finally make sense to me.

So, I started to become more aware of my surroundings and pay attention to things. I started to declutter my life by removing people and things that clouded my vision with self-induced drama that took up a lot of my life by allowing me to become involved in their dramas in the hope that I was helping them. The thing I realized is that everyone shifts into parallel realities, but many do it on auto-pilot, because they're focused on their own unconscious cycle of self-created dramas and often get distracted by other people's dramas. If I declutter my life, then I become self-aware and can stay more focused on how I manifest.

That's the difference between sleep walking and being awake. Often, being involved in other people's dramas where I really was not part of just prevented me from really spending the 24 hours I have every day focusing on the things I wanted to manifest for myself. Now, I attentively listen to the issues people have and make genuine recommendations. Then, I purge myself of what I heard and choose not to be part of it by volunteering my time and energy into participating in fueling their drama by psychologically lending my attention and energy into their issues, which only fuels more of the distress for them. I started to see that I was spending 2 hours here on someone's issues and 3 hours there to do things to help them and before I knew it, I spent half my day invested in their life issues and not involved in my own life.

    I was emotionally exhausted by allowing myself to be the garbage dump for other people's drama. I saw that much of my day was living other people's lives and not mine. How much of my life am I living? That's when I realized, I was suffering by not accepting people as they are and often these people create their own suffering. I was suffering by needing fulfillment in being the hero to other people who often manifest new dramas afterward. I realized that some people are addicted to suffering as they thrive in getting rescued by others and I was not helping them at all by enabling them to continue to be the victim of their circumstances. If I truly loved them, then I must love them enough to let them fall so they can pick themselves up. I help where I can and if it is shown that I need to remove myself from associating with such people who use good people as a crutch to not help themselves, then I politely exit the stage and cheer them on from afar.

    I stopped feeling guilty for not spending much of my time helping people who seem to have issues in their lives that after further inspection are often self-induced over a series of decisions, they made that compounded upon one another, which lead to the outcome they are crying for help about. Like a drug, I was just pacifying their pain. When I stopped helping them over and over again, they finally felt the pain and some start to tend to their own wounds and some wouldn't, because they have not hit their bottom yet. Even if my loved ones became even more self-destructive without me trying to always help them and pushing solutions on them, I learned to separate myself from their dramas and not let them quilt me into continuing to enable their bad habits by being their crutch that they can always relay on to rescue them. Some people do not learn and become a sad story for others to learn from.

Many other people eventually learn from a life of hard knocks, because they finally burned all their bridges with people that when they got their life together, even those people no longer want much a relationship rekindled with them. With the new lessons learned, these people build new bridges and relationships. Many had such horrific experiences that are burned into their psyche and as a result build better relationships and take more accountability for their life for the better. That realization was when I started to really live my life and manifest the reality I wanted to engage in without guilt for being successful in the pursuits I worked at. That was my first major lesson I learned that changed my reality that I am self-aware of.

When I started to practice being conscious of the choices I make and take note of changes in my environment that were different from how I remembered them to be before, I noticed a change. I began to diagnose what I changed my perspective on that I was dealing with recently before the changed reality happened. When I started to do that exercise, I experienced firsthand how my decisions and actions about anything I was working with in my personal life, in my work life, in my artistic hobbies, and especially in my various relationships with friends and family shaped the experiential reality I live in.

My life was becoming the artwork that I studied in my childhood. At first, it was hard to just accept the new realities I was manifesting into as things and people changed or did not exist. I eventually realized that we all live in our own holodecks and my conscious was instantly moving into another version of myself that pre-existed in the new higher or lower level parallel reality. I continue to integrate and just accept everyone as they are and take them seriously no matter how much changed. If I spoke to someone who remembers something different from how I remembered it, then I asked them to explain what happened and I just winged it and went along with it if it suited me or I choose to not go along with it. The decisions I make continue to move me into different parallel realities that are higher or lower based on my decisions. I access and reasscess my reality and tweak my perspective as I move forward in life.

    As a result of becoming more conscious of how my decisions affect the reality I exist in, I started to notice that my dormant 6th senses started to get activated. I started to wonder about that. I asked a monk at one of my mother's Buddhist temples she attends and he said that if I have a gift and use that against people for my own gain, then I would not continue to grow spiritually as I am letting my gifts become accessories to feeding a growing ego that likes to use the new skills I acquired to get adoring followers and possibly admiration from others. It would be like if you were a tall person who could easily reach for fruit that was much higher up on the tree to help someone who is shorter and could not reach the hanging fruit.

    The other choice for this tall person is to use their height as an advantage to pick much of the fruit hanging higher up and leave the barren leaves with very few fruits left on it for the shorter people thus making this person a bully and not a spiritual person. There are graceful decisions you can make with the advantages you have earned. This tall person can work with the shorter people to pick fruit together and cash in on the harvest as a team instead of as competitors. The outcome would be that everyone wins in this scenario. Once your pineal gland is active, then do not let it calcify. I have come across people who are telepathic due to becoming conscious. Personally, telepathy beyond basic communication like having a verbal chat with someone is fine.

    Yet, if you go beyond that and start to read other people's minds without their permission, then it's intrusion of privacy. That's rude and not polite. That's bullying and not spiritual etiquette. You want to treat others as equals, cause if you take advantage of them using your 6th senses than your just fulfilling your ego's desire to control and overpower others for your own gain, which will stunt you spiritually in terms of universal growth. The universe does not reward bullies. Those types of relationships where you forced people to do as you told them to do are not real, just artificial. You can't make people be your friends. You can't make people love you. If you could, you wouldn't want to.

The real thing that's genuine and not artificial is where the lessons are learned and you grow spiritually from it. Genuine relationships of love are where you will grow from, not artificial ones. That's why many people who have 6th senses often withhold them so that they do not feed their ego's desire for admiration and fake relationships. Our relationships with people, with money, with our careers, and many other types of relationship are where we learn and grow from spiritually. You can fake your relationships, but the universe knows what's genuine and won't let you pass into the next level of existences and new experiences that could be open to you. A truly wise person would see others as equals and teach where able to so that they can someday teach others what they know and on and on the lessons are learned.

In esoteric beliefs, your reality is reflections of decisions you made that you are experiencing currently. The decisions and actions you make today will propel your consciousness into the next parallel reality that fits your new vibration. What many practicing Buddhists dislike is repeating the same suffering over and over again not knowing what decisions they made that is manifesting the same similar outcomes they are experiencing? Groundhogs day of repeating the same lessons are what many Buddhist believe is hell if hell truly exists. As your reality are reflections of your beliefs.

    One can manifest a treacherous hell and demonic inhabitants to be as real as they want it to be to justify their own belief in a system of self-punishment for eternity for making poor decisions in one lifetime. Taking a moment to think about that statement makes it seem illogical to believe in such existences. My idea of hell is reincarnating with the same bipolar parent, because I did not learn to let go of my love ones and let them learn their tough lessons. Instead, I tried to rescue people and do things for them so they never learn over and over again, lifetime after lifetime until I finally got off that cycle and start to become self-aware. Once I got off the drama train, I learned that the act of a conscious and self-aware person who helps others that suffer by teaching them how to not suffer as much while living as an equal person in this reality is a trait often coined in Buddhism to label such people as Bodhisattvas.

Bodhisattvas know that everyone on Earth, in all dimensions, and all universes are living their pre-planned incarnation to learn and grow or not grow from their life lessons. As life learners, there is no need to convert anyone into anything unless they come to you to learn from you as a requested mentor of a trade or skill that they would like to acquire for themselves so that they can someday teach it to others who request mentorship. The students eventually become the teachers and the teachers eventually become students again and that cycle continues as we evolve spiritually.

This book is my understanding of the Four Noble Truths and Eightfold Path and how I have used it to manifest with. This is my journey of how I became self-aware and manifest my reality I engage with. Like the popular Buddhist chant I've heard thousands of times growing up by the monks, "Om mani padme hum", I wish for all who want to partake in a conscious and self-aware journey to become the embodiment of the chant themselves. "Om mani padme hum" means the jewel in the lotus flower is an enlightened being. The goal of each incarnation with its many lessons is for the person to reveal one leaf at a time, learn one lesson at a time, and leaf after leaf get closer to the center of the lotus flower. The center of the lotus flower is you; you eventually become an enlightened being.

As an enlightened being, you now have what it takes to manifest the reality you want to exist in. And hey, every lotus flower has a little frog sitting on the lotus leaves waiting for the flower to bloom and enjoying the process. The process leads to perfection. You are perfecting your vibration lesson learned after another. My middle name "Kob" is Laos for frog. So, I guess you now have a little frog friend accompanying your journey as you bloom. My wish to you if you choose to is to practice the Four Noble Truths and Eightfold Path techniques, I have outlined so you can start seeing how your decisions manifest new parallel realities. Then you can have your own first-hand experience and understand how you are the cause of the effected reality you interact in. Namaste.

About the Author

Von D. Galt is an author who earned her knowledge of metaphysics and consciousness from her Laotian upbringing in Buddhism. In *"Buddhist Guide to Manifest Parallel Realities: Using the Four Noble Truths and Eightfold Path in the Age of Consciousness"*, readers get insight from her 36 years of experience studying metaphysics of Buddhism. She earned her Bachelor of Arts degree from the University of Washington and earned her MBA in E-Business Management from Westwood College of Technology. Stay tuned for more enlightening books regarding the Buddhist spiritual tradition.

Index

Introduction..1
Chapter 1 Noble Truth #1 Life is Suffering...........14
Suffering is Physical Pain....................................15
Suffering is Emotional Pain 17
Chapter 2 Noble Truth #2 Attachment
Causes Suffering..22
Attachments are Addictions..............................25
Attachment to Expectations..............................28
Attachment to Forms..31
Attachment to Things...36
Chapter 3 Noble Truth #3 Insights
Remove Suffering..38
Chapter 4 Noble Truth #4 Living the Eightfold
Path Ends Suffering...44
Chapter 5 Eightfold Path.....................................50
Correct Thought...51
Correct Speech...53
Correct Action..56
Correct Livelihood...56
Correct Understanding.......................................59
Correct Effort...63
Correct Concentration..64
Correct Mindfulness..67
Chapter 6 Applying the Principles.....................73
Matrix of Delusion Worksheet...........................82
Conclusion..190
About the Author 213

Bibliography

Buddha. (n.d.). BrainyQuote.com. Retrieved February 19, 2016, from BrainyQuote.com Web site: http://www.brainyquote.com/quotes/authors/b/buddha
Read more at http://www.brainyquote.com/citation/quotes/authors/b/buddha#H4J2MJWzBs5UPXP6.99

Made in the USA
Las Vegas, NV
16 January 2021